BIG BANG

The Loud Debate
Over Gun Control

Norman L. Lunger

Twenty-First Century Books · Brookfield, Connecticut

Cover photograph courtesy of PhotoEdit

Photographs courtesy of PhotoEdit: pp. 10 (© A. Ramey), 12 (© Steven Lunetta), 14 (© Mark Richards), 37 (© Mark Richards), 64 (© Paul Conklin), 70 (© Cleve Bryant), 76 (top © Rachel Epstein; bottom © Mary Kate Denny); © AFP/Corbis: p. 18; AP/Wide World Photos: pp. 21, 84; Stock Boston: pp. 26 (© Bob Daemmrich), 42 (© Joe Sohm); TimePix: pp. 34 (© Shelly Katz), 38 (© Taro Yamasaki), 110 (© Loomis Dean), 130 (© Steve Liss); Photofest: p. 52; Rothco Cartoons: pp. 79 (© Wicks/*The Newhall Signal*, 1989), 82 (© Baloo); National Archives: p. 92

Quotation on page 6 from Erik Eckholm, "Thorny Issue in Gun Control: Curbing Responsible Owners," *The New York Times*, April 3, 1992, pp. A1 and A15.

Library of Congress Cataloging-in-Publication Data
Lunger, Norman L.
Big bang : the loud debate over gun control / Norman L. Lunger.
p. cm.
Includes bibliographical references and index.
ISBN 0-7613-2260-4 (lib. bdg.)
1. Gun control—United States—Juvenile literature. 2. Firearms—Law and legislation—United States—Juvenile literature. 3. Gun control—Cross-cultural studies—Juvenile literature.   I. Title.
HV7436 .L86 2002   363.3'3—dc21   2001008035

Published by Twenty-First Century Books
A Division of The Millbrook Press, Inc.
2 Old New Milford Road
Brookfield, Connecticut 06804
www.millbrookpress.com

CONTENTS

The Holy Grail of gun control has been to find some way to keep guns out of the hands of the bad guys, yet leave the legitimate firearms-owning population alone.

—James D. Wright, criminologist
The New York Times, April 3, 1992

CHAPTER 1

Dreams and Nightmares

"Man with a gun!"

Those words crackling from a police radio can send adrenaline rushing through police and bystanders alike. Why is the man openly carrying a gun? Is he a terrorist? A hunter returning from the hunt? An angry worker with a grudge against the boss who fired him? A drug dealer bent on blasting a competitor? An undercover police officer stalking a criminal? A movie actor playing a part?

He could be any of those—or something else entirely. But until you know for sure, you'd better use the utmost caution. Guns are deadly weapons, and in the wrong hands they can and do wreak havoc. With alarming fre-

quency, the news brings stories of mass killings by people armed with pistols, shotguns, assault rifles, and even more deadly guns.

The fact is, guns are widely available in the United States today and are used for both legitimate and illegitimate purposes. So how can society assure that guns do not find their way into the wrong hands? How can society protect the rights of legitimate gun users while keeping guns away from those who would misuse them? Those questions are at the center of a noisy debate that has been raging across the United States, dividing Americans along many fault lines.

The debate is about gun control, and it has raised many questions. What, if any, controls should be placed on access to guns? What does the U.S. Constitution say about guns and gun rights? Does the Constitution limit the actions that government can take to control the possession and use of guns? How can we balance a right to live safely with a right to own guns? Could stricter gun controls upset the balance of power between the government and the people, relieving would-be tyrants of the fear that an armed citizenry could rise up and overthrow them? Would gun controls work as intended, or would they backfire and leave armed criminals to prey on an unarmed populace? Those are only a few of the questions the debate has stirred up.

Guns are deeply embedded in American life. They are more widely available in the United States than in any other advanced industrial nation. Many Americans love guns—but many others hate them. Guns are often the objects of people's dreams. Yet they are just as often the stuff of people's nightmares.

A Dream: Let's Go Hunting

Many a child in rural or small-town America awaits the opening day of big-game hunting season with excited anticipation. In many areas it's a day off from school, adding a holiday feeling to the start of the annual autumn hunt.

Full of anticipation, a teenager
learns to use a rifle.

In many families, hunting is a sport that unites people
across gender lines and generations. Dad and Mom hunt
together, and when sons and daughters are old enough,
they, too, join in the hunt. (Some states set a minimum age
for hunting, or require that an adult be present.) Thus,
hunting becomes a rite of passage, an event that marks the
advancement from childhood to adolescence, an initiation
into the mysteries of approaching adulthood.

In some families, hunting is mainly a male ritual.
Women and girls stay home while men and older boys go
off to hunt. Perhaps the hunters stay at a camp that is

shared with relatives and friends. The hunting camp may be a small cabin, chock full of bunk beds, with a wood or propane stove for cooking hearty meals. At night everyone sits around a fire and relives the excitement of the day's hunt—shots made and missed, encounters with other hunters, "big ones" that were bagged or got away. Then it's time for sleep and dreams of the perfect shot that tomorrow's hunt will surely bring.

A Nightmare: Guns and Mayhem

City folk who don't hunt or roam the countryside may have no appreciation of such dreams. For many, the word "gun" has other associations—nightmarish ones. The word may bring to mind a man in a tall tower picking off innocent passersby with well-aimed rifle shots. Or a terrorist gunning down innocent people at an airline check-in counter. Or a pair of troubled teenagers who sneak an arsenal of weapons into a school and methodically massacre classmates and teachers. Or a punk with a pistol who kills a youngster who refuses to give up a gold chain. Or a gathering of young people in someone's home where a careless child picks up a loaded gun and pulls a trigger and kills someone.

News accounts of incidents such as these arouse one's worst fears. So many questions pop into the mind. What if my child visits a friend's home where loaded guns are kept in an unlocked cabinet, and childish curiosity leads to gunplay? What if a classmate takes a gun to school and murders my friend and others in cold blood? What if my mother happens to be on the wrong street at the wrong time and catches a bullet during a shootout between drug dealers or gangs?

**Two gun-wielding young men
attempt a carjacking.**

Dangers lurk in many urban neighborhoods where guns are readily available and are often used for criminal purposes. Adults and children alike are at risk. Children may fear for a parent who works a late shift and returns home through dark and empty streets. Adults may refuse to let children play outside for fear of flying bullets.

A Dream: A Neighborhood Freed From Guns . . . and From Fear

Imagine the "good" dream of a person who lives in one of those dangerous urban neighborhoods. In the sweet dream, the person is walking down her own street on a sunny day, stopping to chat with friendly neighbors, feeling no fear, seeing no sign of crime, no sign of guns, no sign of drugs. What a great feeling to be able to walk the streets unafraid!

This person's dream is of an *absence* of guns. But it is a dream that in many neighborhoods is unlikely to come true.

A Nightmare: Unarmed and Unprotected

We have one more nightmare to consider—the nightmare that haunts many gun owners who count on their guns for protection and who fear that unwise gun-control laws may rob them of their guns, their protection, and their basic rights. They point to nations like Nazi Germany where weapons prohibitions and restrictions paved the way for tyranny and even genocide. Such fears surface in many conversations among gun owners and figure prominently in the debate over gun-control laws. As we will see in later chapters, powerful voices argue that the right to own guns is protected by the U.S. Constitution—and not merely protected but protected absolutely. By this way of thinking, any law that infringes on an individual's right to bear arms—even if it only requires guns to be registered—is unconstitutional. For many who share this point of view, gun control is an instrument of tyranny, and opposing gun control is a civic duty.

Dreams and nightmares, nightmares and dreams. When Americans think about guns, they may be hearing echoes of their fondest dreams or their worst nightmares. No wonder the debate over gun control is both loud and contentious.

Is the debate so loud, so contentious, that there is no hope of bridging the wide differences among Americans, of reaching common ground? It will be the task of this book to explore that question. We will proceed by exploring the role of guns in American society from its earliest days up to the present, and laying out the arguments that make the debate over gun control such an explosive one.

Firebells in the Night

The words crackled from a law-enforcement scanner at 11:21 A.M. on April 20, 1999: *"Shots fired at Columbine High School."* By shortly after noon, fifteen people had been killed and about thirty wounded in a frenetic outburst of gunfire on the 1,800-student campus in Littleton, Colorado, a suburb of Denver.

Two boys—high-school seniors with a liking for black trench coats and shoot-'em-up video games—had brought to school a 9-millimeter semiautomatic rifle, a 9-millimeter semiautomatic pistol, two sawed-off 12-gauge shotguns, thirty pipe bombs, and an immense propane-and-gasoline bomb. At 11:19 A.M., they began gunning down their fellow students.

Students watch in horror as the last of their fellow students are evacuated from Columbine High School following the April 1999 shooting.

Almost immediately, calls began coming in to the 911 emergency center from terrified students using cell phones, some of them hiding in closets to escape the mayhem. By 11:29 A.M., eight minutes after the first alarm, police officers began to arrive at the school. Then came SWAT teams—special weapons and tactics units—to try to flush out the gunmen and evacuate the students. TV-station helicopters and news vans showed up to begin live coverage of the gripping drama. Among other things, viewers saw panicky students with faces pressed against school windows, desperately seeking a way of escape. Five hours passed before the police were satisfied that the danger was past. The shooters were dead at their own hands.

Also dead were twelve other students and a teacher. Had the shooters succeeded in efforts to set off their bombs, the toll undoubtedly would have been much higher.

The Columbine school massacre evoked dread and foreboding throughout the land. The shootings would have been shocking enough if they had been unique, an isolated outburst of blood-curdling violence. But fatal gunfire had shattered the peace of other schools before Columbine. In the previous school year, 1997–1998, school shootings had struck Pearl, Mississippi (two dead); West Paducah, Kentucky (three dead); Jonesboro, Arkansas (five dead); Edinboro, Pennsylvania (one dead); Fayetteville, Tennessee (one dead); and Springfield, Oregon (two dead). Still more shootings were to follow. Scarcely a month after Columbine, a fifteen-year-old boy carrying a .22-caliber rifle and a handgun shot and wounded six students at Heritage High School in Conyers, Georgia. In March 2000, a six-year-old boy took a handgun to school and killed a first-grade classmate in Flint, Michigan. Since then, still other schools have experienced gunfire and death.

Outrage and Debate

As typically happens after school shootings, the tragedy at Columbine High aroused outrage and debate. In this case, national attention focused on two issues: the entertainment industry's fascination with gun violence, and the ready availability of guns in U.S. society.

Critics lambasted violent movies and television dramas, saying they created an atmosphere in which murderous violence seems a normal way to settle problems and resolve personal conflicts. A special target of criticism after Columbine was the video-game industry for making games such as "Doom," a favorite of one of the shooters. Players of "Doom" wield high-powered virtual guns as they maneuver through a maze, trying to blast away evil enemies. Announcing an investigation of violence in entertainment two months after Columbine, President Bill Clinton called attention to ads for video games that summoned players to "get in touch with your gun-toting, cold-blooded murdering side" and to "kill your friends guilt free."[1] "I know this stuff sells," said Clinton, "but that doesn't make it right."

Supporters of gun control capitalized on the reaction against Columbine, which resulted in polls indicating that 80 percent of Americans favored stricter gun controls. The Clinton administration submitted new gun bills to Congress, including a measure aimed at stiffening penalties for adults who supply handguns to juveniles. The Columbine shooters got older acquaintances to supply them with guns at a time when neither was yet eighteen, the minimum age under federal law for buying a rifle or shotgun or possessing a handgun. Gun-control advocates also pushed for laws to extend background checks on gun buyers to cover sales by private collectors at weekend gun shows. All four guns used in the Columbine shootings had been bought at gun shows and then passed on to the killers. Every state conducts background checks for sales by licensed gun dealers at stores or gun shows, but sales by private individuals who are not engaged in the business of gun retailing are often exempt from such checks, whether the sale takes place in a living room or at a gun show. The year after Columbine, in November 2000, Colorado and Oregon voters approved statewide initiatives requiring background checks for private sales at weekend shows, and Congress began considering a federal law along the same lines.

While people of all political persuasions have been horrified by school shootings, many people reject the idea that stiffer gun controls are the answer. Supporters of gun rights argue, for example, that stricter enforcement of existing laws and tougher measures against those who use guns to commit crimes are better ways of securing public safety. Charlton Heston, who heads the pro-gun National

During the NRA's annual meeting in Denver, CO, in May 1999, Charlton Heston, the group's president, said gun owners were not to blame for the Columbine and other school shootings.

Rifle Association (NRA), strongly criticized politicians and the media in the weeks after Columbine for trying to paint gun-rights advocates as bad guys. "The dirty secret of this day and age," he told NRA members in Denver, "is that political gain and media ratings all too often bloom upon fresh graves."[2]

Defense Against Tyranny

To gun-rights supporters, there are many causes for outrage that have nothing to do with terroristic rampages by enraged youths or adults. Abusive actions by federal and state authorities have angered many gun enthusiasts and convinced them that widespread citizen possession of firearms is the only sure way to defend against tyranny.

Two events in the 1990s helped to solidify this conviction. One was the killing of a boy and his mother during a standoff at Ruby Ridge, in Idaho's Selkirk Mountains, between federal agents and a former Green Beret named Randall "Randy" Weaver. The other was an explosion and fire that killed some eighty people, including twenty-five children, who were members of the Branch Davidian religious sect, when an army of FBI agents besieged their compound outside Waco, Texas.

The events at Ruby Ridge had their origins in 1989, when a man working undercover for the Bureau of Alcohol, Tobacco and Firearms (BATF) persuaded Randy Weaver to sell him two sawed-off shotguns. Under federal law, any shotgun shorter than 18 inches (45.7 centimeters) is heavily restricted, and these guns were 17¾ inches long. The government apparently hoped to use the threat of a firearms charge to persuade Weaver to work undercover to gather information about a white-supremacist

group called the Aryan Nations, whose gatherings he and
his family had attended. Weaver refused to cooperate and
was charged with illegal shotgun sales. When he failed to
show up for a court hearing or respond to court orders,
U.S. marshals staked out his isolated cabin on Ruby
Ridge. Rather than try to arrest a man they knew to be
well armed and unwilling to surrender, the marshals just
waited. And waited. And waited—for well over a year.
Meanwhile, friends kept Weaver, his wife Vicki, and their
four children supplied with food.

Then, on August 21, 1992, the marshals quietly moved
in on the Weavers. In the woods near the cabin, three marshals armed with automatic weapons encountered
Weaver, his fourteen-year-old son Sam, Sam's dog, and an
adult friend named Kevin Harris. Gunshots rang out.
(There was conflicting testimony about who shot first.)
Soon the dog, Sam Weaver, and a deputy marshal lay
dead. Randy Weaver and Harris carried Sam's body back
to the cabin and prepared to withstand a siege.

With a law officer dead, what had been an illegal gun
sale case would be treated as a murder case. The federal
government rushed in FBI and BATF agents to back the
marshals. Idaho supplied state police officers and members of the Idaho National Guard. Local law officers were
on hand, too. Federal agents received shoot-to-kill orders
applying to any armed adult.

On August 22, an FBI sniper fired a rifle shot that
passed through the curtained window of the cabin door
and killed Vicki Weaver, Randy's wife, as she stood in the
doorway holding their infant daughter. The shot also
wounded gun-carrying Kevin Harris, the man the agent
claimed he was aiming at. Randy Weaver was shot in the
arm about the same time. The siege continued for another

nine days before Weaver and his three surviving children agreed to surrender. (Harris gave himself up a day earlier.)

Supporters of gun rights were in the forefront of those who voiced outrage at the federal role in the long chain of events now known as "Ruby Ridge." They accused the government of setting up Weaver on the gun charge. They claimed the government targeted him solely because of his white-separatist beliefs and his deep suspicion of government. They said the federal government tampered with evidence and tried to cover up some of its actions in the case—charges the government later admitted.

An Idaho jury eventually found Randy Weaver innocent of the gun charge that started it all, while convicting him of failing to appear in court and violating bail conditions. A federal jury found Weaver and Harris not guilty of killing the deputy marshal, accepting their claim that they acted in self-defense. Weaver and his children filed a civil lawsuit against the federal government for the deaths of Vicki and Samuel, a suit that the government eventually settled by paying $3.1 million. Harris also filed a civil suit and received $380,000.

If the deaths of a handful of people at Ruby Ridge in 1992 had caused alarm, the far greater toll near Waco the following year proved an even greater provocation to many people. Once again, guns figured in the equation. David Koresh, the leader of the religious group known as Branch Davidians, was suspected of having an "arsenal" of illegal weapons that included semiautomatic rifles illegally converted to automatic. Expecting trouble, the BATF sent seventy-six agents to arrest Koresh on February 28, 1993. They came heavily armed to the isolated compound—a grouping of several farm buildings—where Koresh lived with the men, women, and children who were his followers. A gun battle erupted in which four fed- eral agents and six of Koresh's followers died.

Once again, federal agents began a siege, hoping to persuade women and children at least to leave the compound. This siege lasted fifty-one days. On April 19, 1993, the FBI gave the Branch Davidians one last chance to come out. Then armored vehicles advanced toward the buildings and knocked holes in the walls so that a potent tear gas could be sprayed inside. Fires broke out in at least three places, creating a holocaust in which Koresh and about eighty men, women, and children died.

Years of recriminations followed, including charges that the FBI had started the fires deliberately, using incendiary devices. When evidence emerged that incendiary tear-gas canisters had indeed been used, despite FBI denials at the time, the government appointed a special counsel to investigate. The counsel's report in July 2000 concluded that the incendiary devices had been used several hours before the fires broke out and could not have been responsible—although he also criticized the government for confusion and lack of candor. A civil lawsuit filed by survivors of those killed in the fires was decided in favor of the government two months later. A federal judge ruled that federal agents acted lawfully and in response to gunfire from both male and female residents of the Branch Davidian compound.

Those findings did little to calm the fears of those who saw the Waco events as an outrageous example of government abuse against ordinary citizens. One who held such a view was Gulf War veteran Timothy J. McVeigh, who told his sister that BATF agents were nothing but "power-hungry storm troopers." McVeigh was in Waco during the fifty-one-day siege and watched parts of the standoff from

The BATF: Jack-booted Thugs or Thwarted Heroes?

BATF agents on the grounds around the Branch
Davidian compound during the 1993 standoff

To many opponents of gun control, the men and women of the
BATF are a group of "jack-booted thugs" who spend their
working hours harassing gun owners and gun dealers. To many
supporters of gun control, the same men and women are wor-
thy people whose heroic efforts to enforce the nation's gun
laws are thwarted at every turn by a Congress that is "under the
thumb of the gun lobby."

One agency. Two wildly contrasting views.

Created in 1972 as an arm of the Treasury Department, the
BATF is the main agency responsible for enforcing federal gun
laws (as well as enforcing the collection of alcohol and tobacco
taxes). Its agents issue permits for the manufacture and import
of guns. They license gun dealers and check to see that they are

complying with federal laws. They try to thwart gun smugglers. They also trace guns used in crimes to find where, when, and by whom they were purchased.

The powers of the BATF have been carefully hemmed in with legislative restrictions, and its staff has been held to roughly 1,600 agents, or one-third the size of the Drug Enforcement Administration (DEA). Unlike the DEA, which has strong support in Congress, the BATF is more likely to be vilified than praised. "Everything we touch is unpopular and controversial," BATF director John W. McGaw told *The New York Times* in 1999. "So we have to be very careful to do what Congress has decided we should and be neutral regulators, not take sides in the gun debate."[3]

Among the outspoken critics of the BATF are leaders of the NRA, the largest organization (more than 4 million members) representing U.S. gun owners and gun enthusiasts. NRA chief executive officer Wayne R. LaPierre included a chapter on "BATF Abuses" in his 1994 book *Guns, Crime, and Freedom*. He opened the chapter with a quote from a Democratic member of Congress, John D. Dingell of Michigan, who said in 1980: "If I were to select a jack-booted group of fascists who were perhaps as large a danger to American society as I could pick today, I would pick BATF. They are a shame and a disgrace to our country."[4] Dingell had further acid criticisms of the bureau after Waco.

From the NRA's perspective, much of what the BATF does is suspect. In his book, LaPierre accuses the BATF of "manufacturing criminals" by "creating phoney gun law violations to justify its existence."[5] He cites a report by the Senate Judiciary Committee in the 1980s that accused the agency of prosecuting dealers for minor technical points and violating gun enthusiasts' constitutional rights.[6] More recently, when BATF agents have run "stings" aimed at catching gun dealers who supply weapons to career criminals, the NRA has accused them of harassing honest gun dealers and legitimate gun buyers by trying to entrap them into violations. LaPierre says the bureau should go after street criminals and their gun suppliers, not legitimate gun dealers. "The government," he says, "has every statute it needs to stop the bad guys, and when they don't, I think they are just playing politics."[7]

The BATF says that a large proportion of guns that are used in crimes can be traced to a handful of unscrupulous gun dealers. According to a study the agency did in the 1990s, 57 percent of all guns used in crimes could be traced to 1,020 dealers, or just 1.2 percent of gun dealers. For a typical "sting," BATF agents might have a convicted criminal go to a gun dealer and try to buy a gun. Under federal law, dealers are forbidden to sell guns to felons, so if a sale is made, the BATF can file charges against the dealer. Under federal court rulings, BATF agents are barred from posing as criminals themselves.

The NRA has considerable clout in Congress, thanks to its large membership and its extensive lobbying efforts. Over the years, the organization has succeeded in whittling down the bureau's powers. For example, the NRA spearheaded the Firearms Owners Protection Act of 1986, which set a one-per-year limit on the number of inspections BATF agents can make of a gun dealer's accounts. (The limit does not apply if there is sound reason to suspect the dealer of criminal activity.) The law also eased off on gun dealers who fail to keep proper records, reducing record-keeping violations from a felony (serious crime) to a misdemeanor (lesser crime). The 1986 law also made it harder for the government to win convictions of gun dealers who supply weapons to criminals or "straw purchasers" (people who buy guns on behalf of others). The law now requires prosecutors to prove not only that dealers made such sales but also that they did so "knowingly and willfully."

The BATF also operates under other restrictions set by Congress. For example, it cannot maintain a computerized record of gun sales. And it can regulate sales only by licensed firearms dealers, not private individuals.

Defenders of the BATF argue that such restrictions tie the agency's hands and prevent it from effectively enforcing the law. David Kennedy, a university researcher involved in efforts to block gun trafficking in Boston, has called BATF agents "heroes." He told *The New York Times*: "The only fair thing to say is that they have been systematically kept away from doing a vitally important job."[8]

Frederick S. Calhoun, a historian, links the BATF's February 1993 raid on the Branch Davidian compound near Waco to a longstanding interest of the federal government in countering organized groups that collect large arsenals that might be used against private citizens or the government. From Shays's Rebellion in 1786-1787 to the present, government agencies have sought to forbid such private arsenals, Calhoun argues—although there are no laws against owning a large number of guns. Calhoun cites a series of violent confrontations between the government and groups on both the right and left sides of the political spectrum that have stockpiled weapons and used them for bank robberies and assassinations. In the 1970s, federal and local agents tracked members of the radical leftist Symbionese Liberation Army (SLA) to a house in the Watts section of Los Angeles. In a shootout, all six SLA members in the house—including the group's top leaders—were killed. (The SLA had used assassination and kidnapping in seeking to advance a black-power agenda. The group kidnapped publishing heiress Patricia Hearst, who then took part in an SLA bank robbery, for which she served three years in prison.)

In the 1980s, a right-wing, white-power group known as The Order amassed a private armory and used it to assassinate Alan Berg, a Jewish talk-show host in Denver; bomb a Boise synagogue; and rob armored cars. The group's take had reached $2 million by the time the FBI surrounded its hideout in 1984, killed its leader, and sent other members to prison. More recently, the BATF has kept a close watch on the so-called militia movement, in which armed groups organize for all-out war as a last resort to defend against what they regard as threats to their liberties and rights.

So are BATF agents thugs or heroes? Are the laws under which they operate too permissive—or too restrictive? The answers tend to depend on who's talking and how the speaker feels about gun control and the trustworthiness of the federal government.

a nearby hill. There he sold anti–gun-control bumper stickers with messages like "Fear the government that fears your gun," "Ban guns: make the streets safe for a government takeover," and "A man with a gun is a citizen. A man without a gun is a subject." Resentment simmered in McVeigh's mind. On April 19, 1995, two years to the day after the Waco holocaust, he tried to get even by exploding a powerful truck bomb that destroyed the federal building in Oklahoma City. His main target was a BATF office on the ninth floor. The blast—the worst act of domestic terrorism ever carried out on U.S. soil by a U.S. citizen—killed 168 people, including 19 children at a day-care center for federal employees. McVeigh was later convicted of murder and conspiracy and executed by lethal injection.

The violence and passion that have marked the American debate over guns grow out of the "culture wars" that divide Americans along many fault lines and on many issues. In these "wars," the basic split is between, on the one hand, those who feel a commitment to what they see as valuable traditions that are under challenge in modern society and, on the other hand, those who welcome many of the changes in society as evidence of an evolving social conscience. Gun-rights supporters tend to be in the first group—deeply suspicious of "big government" and seeing the Second Amendment as an example of a tradition that is under attack. Gun-control supporters tend to be in the second group—seeing guns as a menace to health and safety and believing that guns must be brought under control through the use of the regulatory powers of government.

A number of organized interest groups help to stoke the fires of the debate over guns and gun control. The following table lists some of the leading players. Many have Web sites where they explain their perspectives and set forth their positions on current gun-related issues. (Web addresses may change. If you have trouble accessing any of the sites below, use a search site like www.google.com and search using the organization's name within double quotes.)

Groups Critical of Gun Control

Citizens Committee for the Right to Keep and Bear Arms
    www.ccrkba.org/
Firearms.org
    www.firearms.org/
Gun Owners of America
    www.gunowners.org/
Jews for the Preservation of Firearms Ownership
    www.jpfo.org/
KeepandBearArms.com
    www.keepandbeararms.com/
Mothers Arms
    www.mothersarms.org/
National Rifle Association (NRA)
    www.mynra.com
National Shooting Sports Foundation
    www.nssf.org/
Pink Pistols
    www.pinkpistols.org/
Second Amendment Foundation
    www.saf.org/
Second Amendment Police Department
    www.paulrevere.org/

Second Amendment Sisters
    www.sas-aim.org/
Women Against Gun Control
    wagc.com/index.html

Groups Supportive of Gun Control

Americans for Gun Safety
    ww2.americansforgunsafety.com/
Brady Campaign to Prevent Gun Violence
    www.bradycampaign.org/
Brady Center to Prevent Handgun Violence
    www.bradycenter.org/
Coalition to Stop Gun Violence
    www.gunfree.org/
Firearms Litigation Clearinghouse
    www.firearmslitigation.org/
Million Mom March (affiliated with Brady Campaign)
    www.millionmommarch.com/
Mothers Against Guns
    mothersagainstguns.org/
PAX
    www.paxusa.org/
Sane Guns
    www.saneguns.org/
Violence Policy Center
    www.vpc.org/
Violence Prevention Research Program
    web.ucdmc.ucdavis.edu/vprp/

Arming America

Some people hang them on a rack behind the driver's seat in their pickup trucks, where they can be easily reached if a coyote or deer comes into sight. Some slip them into a handbag for protection. Some strap them in a holster beneath their suit jacket or on their hip. Some stuff them in the glove compartment or beneath the driver's seat in their car. Some store them in glass-fronted gun racks in their den, or mount them over a fireplace.

Guns seem to be everywhere in the United States. In a Texas courtroom, a judge took his antique revolvers apart to repair them while presiding over jury selection in a capital murder case. When reprimanded by a state commis-

Most gun shops in America offer a
vast array of weapons—from hunting rifles
to handguns to semiautomatics.

sion, the judge remarked: "Almost all the judges carry guns. I just should have kept mine under the robe instead of outside of it with a screwdriver."

More people own guns in the United States than in any other country in the world. At last count, more than 230 million firearms were believed to be in the possession of U.S. residents, and U.S. factories were churning out four or five million more each year. Guns are present in approximately four out of every ten households. The figures on possession are not too precise, one should note, since some gun owners will not reveal private information to pollsters and the U.S. government is prohibited by law from keeping a registry of guns or gun ownership. That is due largely to the power of the gun lobby, which will be discussed in Chapter 4.

People Who Own Guns

People who own guns tend to fall into two groups: utilitarians and romantics. Utilitarians value a gun for its utility, its usefulness. A woman may carry a handgun in her purse, planning to use it only if she has to defend herself. She'll hardly think of it in the meantime. A terrorist with assassination in mind will choose a precision weapon with just the right characteristics for the job. Romantics, on the other hand, value a gun not just for its usefulness or firepower but also for some deeper value—its link to childhood memories, its place in the history of firearms, its rarity, its flat-out beauty. Romantics are downright gun lovers. As online hunting columnist Russ Chastain writes: "I long ago adopted my father's motto: 'If it shoots, I like it.' . . . I love guns like some folks love fishing rods, others love cars, and still others go nuts for football."[1]

Beyond these two overarching groups, gun owners tend to fall into seven basic (but overlapping) categories:

1. *Hunters.* Outside of major metropolitan cities, in the small towns and rural hinterlands of America, hunting is a widely popular sport participated in by as many as 17 million Americans. "I can't imagine not hunting. It's like breathing," one Montanan told the *Christian Science Monitor.* The states with the most hunters are Michigan, Texas, Pennsylvania, Wisconsin, and New York.[2]

2. *Those who own guns for self-protection.* A businessperson who regularly carries large sums of money may feel safer carrying a gun. A prominent politician who is constantly in the public eye and has made many enemies may go armed. So may people who feel vulnerable for various reasons—perhaps they have a small physique or a physical infirmity, perhaps they fear abuse because they are gay or belong to a racial or religious minority, perhaps they live on a lonely road far from sources of help. Many people share the feeling of a Virginia woman who told ABC News that she felt she could not count on the police and it was therefore a "really wonderful feeling to know that I have a gun to protect myself."[3]

3. *Gun collectors.* Many enthusiasts have assembled collections of fifty or more firearms of varying vintages and models. Collectors have their own journals and magazines in which they can read about rare and unusual guns. They may frequent gun shows to seek out firearms that will fill gaps in their own collection or that they can resell for a profit. Or they go online to seek out Internet sites at which guns are auctioned. Guns with a unique history can fetch very high prices, such as the $25,875 paid in 1998

for a Smith & Wesson firearm used to kill a notorious bank bandit, John Dillinger, in a 1934 police ambush. Gun collecting is not without its risks, of course, since large arsenals can attract thieves. An Arkansas gun collector lost seventy handguns, rifles, and shotguns valued at $60,000 in 1994 in what prosecutors said was a robbery by an associate of Timothy McVeigh to help finance the Oklahoma City bombing.

4. *Target shooters.* Young people may take up target shooting in order to win badges and advancement in groups such as the Boy Scouts. For many, the sport becomes a lifelong interest. They make regular trips to shooting ranges—found in many towns and cities—to keep their skills and their guns from getting rusty. From

Target shooting is growing in popularity among men and women alike.

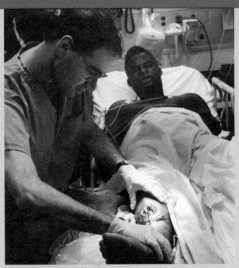

An ER doctor in Chicago inspects the wounded leg of a gunshot victim.

The first gunshot victim rolls through the emergency room door shortly after 9 P.M., and others will follow as the night wears on. It's Saturday night in a public hospital in big-city America, and the trauma team is braced for the inevitable gunshot and stabbing victims. "The Knife and Gun Club" is what trauma specialists call their weekend vigil—and nowadays the wounds are more often from gunshots than from knives.

Bullets can cause awesome damage to the human body. A large-caliber handgun like a .45 can send a slug ripping straight through the torso, leaving a gaping exit hole as it passes out. If it hits a vital organ, there will be a bloody mess and probably a dead person. If it hits a bone, the bone will shatter and bone splinters will dig into nearby muscles and nerves. A smaller slug like a .22 won't make such a big hole, but it could very well cause equal or greater damage. That's because its light weight and high velocity allow it to be deflected by limb or skull bones, causing it to skip around the body like a steel ball in a pinball machine.

Then there are the scattershot wounds from semiautomatic rifles and revolvers, which fire a rapid series of bullets, as fast as a shooter can pull the trigger. If one bullet wound is a mess, four or five can be a disaster. The more slugs that slam into a body, the greater the chance the victim will die or end up a paraplegic, without the use of arms or legs or both. Since the early 1990s, experts say, semiautomatics have replaced small pistols ("Saturday night specials") as the most popular urban weapon.

Gunshot victims tend to be young. (Those most at risk are between the ages of fifteen and twenty-four.) They may be drug peddlers or other criminals who have tangled with a rival or a disgruntled partner. Or they may be victims of a "lovers' quarrel," shot by a spouse or companion in a moment of anger. Others are innocent bystanders struck by gunfire in which they were not involved. Still others are clerks and store owners who were the target of a robbery. Yet others are barroom brawlers. Or victims of road rage. Or police officers shot in the line of duty.

With guns readily available on urban streets, and with drug wars commonplace in recent years, city hospitals have noticed that many gunshot victims are repeaters. Victims who get patched up one night reappear weeks or months later with fresh wounds from a new shooting. "You know it's bad when they start coming back," an emergency room physician told the *Philadelphia Daily News*. At one Philadelphia hospital, 20 percent of gunshot patients are second-timers.[4]

The cost of caring for gunshot victims is immense. If a victim is DOA (dead on arrival) or dies on the operating table soon after being admitted, the bill at one big-city hospital is $3,000. If the victim survives (as three out of four do) and then must undergo months or years of treatment, the cost soars as high as hundreds of thousands of dollars. The typical gunshot victim has no health insurance, so hospitals get stuck with about 80 percent of the costs themselves. Ultimately, those costs—roughly $4 billion a year—are passed on to the taxpayer or buyer of health insurance. In other words, we all end up paying.

"Saturday Night in the ER" is definitely not a free show.

1905 until the 1960s, the U.S. government's civilian marksmanship program supplied surplus rifles and ammunition (for little or no cost) to target-shooting groups affiliated with the National Rifle Association. That assistance dwindled to a trickle in the 1960s, when officials became aware that black militants and white paramilitary groups were among the beneficiaries.

5. *People whose careers require them to carry guns.* These are mainly law-enforcement officers and members of the military, but they also include security guards employed by businesses, housing agencies, and the like. In many cities, police officers are required to carry their weapon even when off duty.

6. *Criminals.* Members of this group run the gamut from street thugs and drug dealers to the shady lords of sprawling criminal enterprises like the Mafia. Here, too, we will include terrorists as well as members of paramilitary groups who use their guns to commit crimes against state power, from revolutionaries on the left to religious-oriented racists on the right.

7. *Hobbyists.* These include people such as war reenactors, who use guns in re-creating historical events.

Gun Enthusiasts

To get a bit of the flavor of gun ownership in this sprawling country, let's take a tour of some of the many places where gun-wielding people congregate.

Our first stop is an encampment of Civil War reenactors at the site of the Battle of Gettysburg. Each year on the anniversary of that battle in late June and early July, reenactors flock to the battlefield in southern Pennsylvania to replay the historic event. People come by the hundreds—men and sometimes women in uniforms of both the Confederacy and the Union, plus women and children in Civil War–era civilian dress. Families pitch tents and gather around campfires at dusk and dawn. Vendors offer a vast range of Civil War–era products, from canvas braces (suspenders) and homespun undershirts to muskets and bayonets.

Reenactors assume the roles of competing military units and act out battles step-by-step, charging across the same hills and valleys that the Blues and the Grays fought over so long ago. Those portraying soldiers carry muskets, rifles, and pistols of the time, which can be bought from various modern-day sutlers (as civilians who supply equipment to the military are known). In addition to guns, a typical sutler's catalog might offer ramrods, powder flasks, shot molds (for making one's own shot), and cartridges, among other accessories. Many reenactors revel in the finer points of nineteenth-century armaments. Some even build their own guns, boring out shafts of steel to make barrels and carving ornate gunstocks out of precious woods.

Reenactment is a popular hobby in many areas, with men and women joining local units like the 8th Ohio Volunteer Infantry or the 1st South Carolina Artillery, patterned on actual units that fought in the war. Gettysburg is only one of dozens of places where reenactors gather. Events take place throughout the year on the anniversaries of battles both famous and obscure, giving participants plenty of opportunity to shoot their guns (using black powder in rolled-paper cartridges without bullets) and practice the art of nineteenth-century warfare. Other reenactors replay other American wars, including the Revolutionary War of 1775–1783.

Our tour takes us next to a "cowboy action shooting" event (or a closely related event featuring "cowboy mounted shooting"). Participants dress up in buckskins, strap on finely tooled holsters and gun belts, and engage in mock gunfights, firing blanks from the kinds of weapons used by real sheriffs and outlaws. Of course, there are cowgirls as well as cowboys, bearing nicknames like "Sawtooth Annie" and "Texas Lily." And some events even feature "shotgun weddings" for a touch of humor.

Enthusiasts call cowboy action shooting "America's fastest growing shooting sport." Clubs exist all over the United States and Canada—not just in western states like

Reenactors assume the stance of cowboys of the Old West.

Arizona and Idaho but also in places like Rhode Island and Alabama. As with Civil War reenactors, shooters replay historic gunfights at annual events like "the Gun-fight at Brawley's Wash" (Tucson, Arizona; January) and "Ambush at Indian Creek" (Donegal, Pennsylvania; Octo-ber). Whereas the goal in Civil War reenactment is to relive a historical moment, cowboy action shooting tests indi-vidual speed and accuracy, and awards go to those who outshoot their rivals. If you need to brush up on your quick-draw techniques or learn the proper way to fall off a horse and come up shooting, you can buy instructional videos and practice at home.

Next our tour takes us to an urban area, where we can visit a busy—and noisy—shooting gallery. Such establish-ments give urban dwellers an opportunity to learn how to hit a target (say, a threatening intruder) or upgrade their marksmanship. An indoor shooting gallery in Orange County, California, advertises "16 lanes, . . . rental guns; .22 rifles ok, no shotguns"—and on Tuesdays, women shoot for free. Outdoor ranges often permit shotguns, carbines, and more powerful weapons.

For beginners, NRA chapters and many other groups offer firearms courses that emphasize basic skills and safety. California is one of several states that requires peo-ple who buy guns to demonstrate that they know how to use them—typically by taking a firearms course and qual-ifying for a certificate of proficiency. While only basic techniques are covered in such beginners' courses, a wide range of more advanced courses can readily be found.

Such courses come in many shapes and sizes. There are courses taught by women for women, often weaving weapons instruction into a more general course on self-protection. There are courses framed as scenarios in

"I Didn't Know the Gun Was Loaded" is the title of an old country-and-western tune, and a sad refrain that investigators hear over and over as they question people involved in accidental shootings. Many of us seem to have an irresistible urge to squeeze triggers—and sometimes that urge costs a life. Statistics show that some four thousand people are shot accidentally each year in the United States, and one out of four of them die. The victims include people like a thirteen-year-old Maryland boy who was shot and killed by a neighbor child who found a gun at home, picked it up, and fired it.

The good news is that accidents involving guns have dropped sharply in recent years, even as the number of guns in circulation has grown. The bad news is that too many people still get hurt or killed this way.

Many accidents happen when hunters mistake a human for a deer or other game animal. To prevent such mistakes, hunters are generally required to wear brightly colored clothing. Blaze orange is easy to see at a distance, and it is definitely not the normal color of a deer. Accidents also happen when someone drops a loaded gun and it goes off—for example, when a hunter is climbing over a fence or trips over a tree root. This is easily prevented by not loading a gun until one is ready to fire, or by activating a safety switch that prevents the gun from going off.

To reduce the number of accidental shootings, many states require people applying for hunting licenses to complete a gun safety course. Some states, including Connecticut and Hawaii, require all gun buyers to complete a safety training course and receive a permit. Most states place additional requirements on children under the age of sixteen who wish to buy a gun or take up hunting.

Gun safety courses are offered by state game departments, schools, civic groups, shooting organizations, and hunters' associations. Many of the courses are free or have a nominal cost. Learning about gun safety is among the requirements for Boy Scouts who seek a merit badge in rifle shooting or shotgun shooting.

Perhaps the best-known sponsor of gun safety courses is the NRA, which offers many types of courses through its state or local affiliates. You can search online at www.mynra.com/ for a list of courses near you. Another place to check is your state's game or wildlife commission.

It's never too early to begin learning about gun safety, since, as we have seen, accidents sometimes occur when small children pick up a gun at home. Both the NRA and the Center to Prevent Handgun Violence offer programs for use in schools, using two distinct approaches.

The NRA program sends police officers and other trainers into classrooms from kindergarten to sixth grade with the message that guns are dangerous and that children should leave them alone. "Stop—Don't Touch—Leave the Area—Tell an Adult," goes the mantra. Sometimes a police officer dons a costume and appears as the program's child-friendly mascot, "Eddie Eagle." Some schools have incorporated the Eddie Eagle program into their health curriculum, alongside sex education and drug-and-alcohol education.

The Center to Prevent Handgun Violence program, targeting children from prekindergarten through high school, takes a different tack. It employs role-playing activities aimed at helping young people learn to manage their anger and develop peaceful ways of resolving conflicts. Trainers discuss the consequences of using guns or other forms of violence in dealing with conflict. They also talk about ways of resisting peer pressure that glorifies guns or violence. This program is dubbed STAR, for Straight Talk About Risks.

Gun Safety Rules

For those who are old enough to use guns responsibly, there are a few basic rules for avoiding harm:

Assume that *every* gun is loaded unless you have just opened it and checked for yourself.

Familiarize yourself with national, state, and local laws about owning and using firearms.

Keep guns and ammunition locked up separately in secure locations when not in use.

Always point a gun in a safe direction—never toward a person, vehicle, or occupied dwelling.

Be sure that there is a backstop behind your target to stop any stray bullet.

Make sure you have the right ammunition for the gun you are using.

Load a gun only when you are ready to use it.

Keep your finger off the trigger until you are ready to shoot.

Never use guns while under the influence of alcohol or drugs.

When carrying a gun, walk—don't run.

Before transporting a gun in a vehicle, remove all cartridges from the gun.

Before cleaning a gun, always verify that it is not loaded.

And, again, assume that *every* gun is loaded unless you have just opened it and checked for yourself.

Remember: "I didn't know the gun was loaded" is *never* a valid excuse.

which learners assume different roles, such as reacting to an ambush. There are courses in how to fire a semiautomatic rifle or a mortar. A sampling of the titles of courses offered by one weapons-instruction company includes: two- and four-day defensive handgun, two-day advanced tactical scenarios, four-day handgun combat, four-day tactical shotgun, four-day precision rifle, two-day submachine gun, and four-day select-fire M16.

After brushing up at one of those courses, a true gun lover might want to attend one of the many shooting matches or "shoots" held on a regular basis in various parts of the country. For example, the three-day Hiram Maxim Machine Gun Shoot in Maine. (The event takes its name from the inventor of the machine gun used in World War I.) Or the enthusiast might want to take part in a shooting competition such as the NRA's National Rifle and Pistol Championships (billed as the "World Series of the Shooting Sports") held each summer at Camp Perry, Ohio, or enter other NRA competitions such as the Silhouette Championships, Collegiate Championships, Black Powder Target Rifle Championships, or Action Shooting Championships.

If you love guns, you'll find plenty of other people out there who share your love.

History of Gun Use

Guns have been a part of American life ever since the first Europeans showed up. Settlers used guns to try to gain an upper hand over Native Americans, first by superior firepower and then by wiles and ruses. A Spanish official, Bernardo de Gálvez, calculated that it made sense to supply Native Americans with guns, since the natives would then "lose their skill in handling the bow" and become dependent on Europeans for ammunition. It never worked out quite that slickly, however, and guns merely provided the Native Americans with one more method for resisting the newcomers.

The uncertainty and danger of life on the frontiers of North America gave settlers a reason for acquiring and learning to use firearms. In Europe, possession of firearms had been a privilege of the upper classes. Here, however, "gentlemen" and commoners alike went armed. The colony of Virginia armed all male residents within four years after its founding in 1607, and following an Indian massacre in 1622, the colony set up an organized militia. From the colonial era through the Civil War, the colony or state militia was the principal military arm of government in North America. At certain times and in certain places, every adult male was required to serve.

As time went on, technological improvements made guns far more reliable and easy to use. At first, guns were so heavy that colonists could not hold them steady—they had to prop the barrel on a forked stick in order to fire the gun. Many of those early guns were matchlock muskets, in which the pulling of a trigger caused a lighted match-cord to dip into a flashpan and touch off an explosive powder that fired the gun. Flintlock muskets were an improvement because they were both lighter and more accurate. They fired by striking flint against steel. Guns grew shorter, too, as they went from 46- and 47-inch (117- and 119-centimeter) barrels to barrels as short as 39 inches (99 centimeters).

With the introduction of rifling, or spiral grooves inside the gun barrel, bullets flew with greater accuracy, and by the time of the U.S. Civil War, the standard small arm was a muzzle-loading rifle (or rifled musket). But muzzle-loaders were slow to load, since gunpowder and shot had to be rammed down the barrel each time the gun was fired. So the next great improvement was the bolt-action breechloader rifle, in which a cartridge containing powder and a bullet was inserted into a chamber at the breech, or rear, of the barrel and locked in by means of a sliding bolt. Before long, inventors had designed repeating rifles, in which several bullets were stored in a chamber and a new shell was inserted in the chamber each time the bolt was pulled back to eject a spent shell.

The next major advance, in the 1880s, was the introduction of smokeless powder, replacing the black powder that not only had produced clouds of smoke but also a residue that fouled gun barrels. Because the new propellant packed three times the power of black powder, it made bullets fly farther and faster and improved shooters' accuracy. By the start of World War I, the United States and other major armies equipped their infantry soldiers with rifles whose barrels were sometimes as short as 24 or 25 inches (61–64 centimeters).

Meanwhile, pistols, too, had been evolving. Abandoning the matchlock and flintlock of earlier, single-shot pistols, Samuel Colt in 1835 patented a revolver (a handgun that held several bullets in a revolving chamber) that fired by means of a pin striking a cartridge. This so-called percussion design (still used today) had been developed a few years earlier for muskets and rifles. A further advance came in 1857 when Smith & Wesson produced a revolver that fired copper cartridges, which were easier and safer to use than older paper cartridges. Pistols were less accurate than rifles and less effective at a distance, but they were convenient to carry and were widely used in the American West.

The twentieth century saw still further developments in gun design, such as semiautomatic rifles and pistols that fired many rounds in rapid succession, each time the trigger was pulled. There were also assault rifles—highly accurate firearms like the Russian AK-47 and the U.S. M16 designed for hitting targets at ranges of up to 300 yards (274 meters). And there was a wide variety of smaller and cheaper guns to appeal to the mass consumer market. Among these were small revolvers (usually .22 caliber) that came to be called "Saturday night specials" because they were sometimes used for quickie holdups and for settling domestic quarrels.

Guns are so much a part of the American fabric that they help to define the United States in the eyes of the world. A Texas teenager who traveled abroad told of meeting strangers who, upon hearing the word "Texas," pointed their hands and pulled an imaginary trigger while remarking knowingly, "Ah, yes, bang, bang—Texas." Guns are also a part of many Americans' self-image. People who have owned and used guns often cannot imagine a world in which they could not bear arms. The widespread admiration—even reverence—for guns makes it extremely difficult to find any common ground between those who want gun control and those who love guns.

CHAPTER 4

Drop It! Now!

On a cold day in February 1929, four men posing as police officers accosted seven men in a Chicago garage, lined them up against a wall, and mowed them down, firing two Tommy guns, a sawed-off shotgun, and a .45 pistol. It was Valentine's Day, and this gruesome mass murder went down in history as the St. Valentine's Day Massacre—a settling of accounts between two gangs of bootleggers, led by Al Capone and George "Bugs" Moran. Although no one ever went to jail for the crime, it was widely attributed to henchmen of Capone. The *rat-a-tat* of Tommy guns (.45-caliber automatic rifles, also known as submachine guns, patented in 1921 by John T. Thompson) had been echoing

Al Capone's henchmen in Hollywood's version
of *The St. Valentine's Day Massacre*,
produced and directed by Roger Corman

through Chicago since 1925, and the St. Valentine's Day Massacre drew attention to the weapon. Although movies sometimes glamorized both bootleggers and Tommy guns, many people were horrified by the lawlessness and the violence. In response to public fears, Congress in 1934 passed the National Firearms Act to regulate and tax the sale of sawed-off shotguns and fully automatic weapons like the Tommy gun.

The National Firearms Act was not the first federal gun-control law, but it was the first one that sought to be comprehensive. It was more sweeping than the earlier Firearms in the Mails Act (1927), which stopped the mailing of concealable firearms to private individuals. As originally introduced, the National Firearms Act would have regulated handguns, too. But a letter-writing campaign spearheaded by the National Rifle Association killed that provision.

That same year, Prohibition, the grand federal experiment in banning alcoholic beverages, came to an end. In the years that followed, bootlegging became less profitable and, thus, less common. But gangsters did not fade away. They shifted their attention to drugs, prostitutes, and other illicit products. And, law or no law, they still armed themselves with Tommy guns and sawed-off shotguns, as well as other high-powered weapons.

Congress took a second crack at comprehensive gun-control in passing the Federal Firearms Act of 1938. Originally designed to require the registration of all handguns and the licensing of their owners, this legislation, too, came under attack by the NRA and was whittled down. In its final form it said nothing at all about handguns. The Federal Firearms Act did just two things: It barred unlicensed dealers from selling guns across state lines, and it banned the sale of firearms to convicted felons and fugitives. But the bill contained a large loophole: It set the fee for a federal gun dealer's license at just $1, so anyone who wanted to buy or sell guns across state lines could easily buy a license and do so legally. (The government eventually concluded that two thirds of those who acquired

If you move to Morton Grove, Illinois, a village outside Chicago, you'll have to leave your pistols behind. Morton Grove adopted an ordinance in 1981 that is one of the toughest gun-control laws in the nation. It bans both *possession* and *ownership* of private handguns within the village limits.

In Kennesaw, Georgia, however, the law takes an opposite tack. If you moved there you would be *required* to own a gun of some sort to assist in the common defense. An ordinance adopted in 1982 requires every head of household to maintain a firearm and keep ammunition for it. The ordinance exempts convicted felons, persons physically unable to use a firearm, people with religious objections, and people too poor to buy a firearm. Such a law is not without precedent. As early as 1632, the Massachusetts Bay Colony insisted that each householder "have . . . a sufficient musket or other serviceable piece for war . . . for himself and each man servant he keeps able to beare arms."

The Morton Grove and Kennesaw ordinances are among more than 20,000 gun laws in effect in the United States today. Federal laws are only a small part of the picture. Each state has its own set of gun laws, and many local governments do, too. Most of those laws deal with such mundane issues as the use of guns in committing a crime (a no-no) or the minimum age for owning a handgun (usually eighteen or twenty-one). But other gun laws, including those mentioned above, stir considerable controversy. Should permits be required for carrying a concealed weapon—and if so, how hard should it be to get a permit? Should there be background checks on purchasers from private individuals at gun shows? These are among the hot-button issues, and they are decided quite differently in different places.

Concealed weapons

In Pennsylvania, except in Philadelphia, it's all right for you to stick a handgun into a holster, strap the holster to your hip, and walk the streets like a gunslinger in the Old West. (Note, however, that you must be age eighteen or over.) But what if you tuck the gun into a pocket where it is no longer visible and then go out in public? That's quite different. It's illegal, unless you have a permit to carry a concealed weapon.

All states except Vermont have concealed-weapons laws, although the specific rules vary. Under a Texas law passed in 1995, state residents can get a permit to carry a concealed weapon after undergoing a background check and ten to fifteen hours of training. In 1997 the law was amended to specify that it is okay to take your concealed weapon into a church or hospital unless the institution expressly forbids it.

A number of states have followed a model concealed-weapons law proposed by the NRA. It requires a "permit to carry," but officials cannot arbitrarily deny a person's application or inquire into the person's reasons for wanting a permit. The permit can be denied only for specific causes such as past violent crimes, pending criminal charges, narcotic use, alien or fugitive status, and commitment to a mental institution or drug-and-alcohol treatment center. Pennsylvania and Texas are among thirty-two states that do not ask an applicant to state a reason for wanting a concealed-weapons permit. Ten other states give local law enforcement discretion in issuing permits. Seven states prohibit the carrying of concealed weapons altogether—Illinois, Kansas, Missouri, Nebraska, New Mexico, Ohio, and Wisconsin.

Background checks

Should background checks be required for purchasers of firearms from private individuals at gun shows—or, more broadly, in any transfer of firearms between private individuals? As we saw earlier, the Columbine High School killers got all four of their guns from individuals who had bought them at gun shows where no background check was required. Colorado has since become one of eleven states that requires background checks on all firearms purchasers at gun shows. The other states are California, Connecticut, Hawaii, Illinois, Maryland, New Jersey, New York, Oregon, Pennsylvania, and Rhode Island.

Say you want to buy a gun from a friend or neighbor. Here's how the law works in Pennsylvania: You cannot (legally) just hand over some money and get the gun. You and the seller must go either to a licensed dealer's gun shop or to a sheriff's office to make the transfer. There, you have to submit to an instant background check before taking ownership of the gun. If you don't pass the background check, you can't buy the gun.

Eighteen states impose waiting periods (ranging from two days to six months) for purchases of firearms. In most cases, this applies to handguns only. However, a few states require waiting periods for purchases of rifles and shotguns, too. Such waiting periods are designed to allow more thorough background checks to take place.

Restrictions on purchases

Another common goal of law-enforcement officials is to stop the sale of firearms to *straw purchasers*, that is, people who buy guns on behalf of others. Often, convicted felons or drug addicts—people not permitted to buy guns themselves—pay straw purchasers to go to a gun dealer and make a legal purchase. Some individuals make a practice of buying guns from dealers in "easy" states and reselling them to gangs in more restrictive states. To limit straw purchases, at least as regards easily concealable handguns, Maryland, California, South Carolina, and Virginia passed "one-handgun-per-month" laws. When you buy a handgun in those states, your name goes into a database and is kept there for thirty days. If you try to buy another gun before the time is up, you will be denied permission.

Comprehensive laws

New York and Massachusetts have gained reputations as the states with the toughest gun laws. New York's 1911 Sullivan Act was the first comprehensive state gun-control law. It required a permit to purchase, possess, or own a handgun. A more recent New York law, adopted in 2000, requires the "ballistic fingerprinting" of new handguns. Before a handgun can be sold in New York, it must be test-fired. Then bullets from the gun and shell casings for those bullets are inspected for distinctive marks. The marks are recorded in a statewide database. (Maryland has a similar law.) New York's 2000 gun-control law also required all new guns to have trigger locks and required gun owners to make a report to police any time a gun is lost or stolen.

Consumer protection laws

Massachusetts blazed new trails by becoming the first state to cover guns under consumer-protection laws. Regulations issued in April 2000 by the state attorney general's office required all guns sold in the state by dealers or manufacturers to have tamper-proof serial numbers, trigger locks, and safety devices that let a user know whether the gun is loaded. The regulations also required devices that make it impossible for handguns to be fired by children under age six. Moreover, guns must have load indicators that show whether or not they are loaded. And they must have a feature that prevents accidental firing if a bullet remains in the chamber after the ammunition magazine has been removed.

Child protection

Massachusetts is among sixteen states that have laws aimed at preventing children from gaining access to firearms. The Massachusetts law (adopted in 1998) requires gun owners to keep their guns in locked cabinets or to have them equipped with childproof and tamper-resistant safety locks.

The amazing differences among state gun laws may seem mind-boggling and confusing. But there is one virtue to such a variety of laws: The states can serve as a testing ground to see how various laws work out in practice.

licenses were not commercial dealers at all. Instead, they were hobbyists buying for themselves and their friends.) Moreover, the ban on sales to criminals set a tough standard of proof, and for thirty years not one dealer was brought to trial for such a sale.

The issue of gun control largely faded from the public consciousness until January 1963, when Senator Thomas Dodd of Connecticut brought it back to life. He began a series of hearings on "crime in the streets" and the role of cheap, imported handguns—"Saturday night specials." His stated goal as chairman of the Senate subcommittee on juvenile delinquency was to make it more difficult for young delinquents to buy cheap guns. But by most accounts Dodd's true aim was to help U.S. gun makers, who were losing market share to inexpensive handguns and surplus military weapons imported from Europe. Gun makers were politically powerful in Dodd's home state of Connecticut, which had long been a main center of the gun industry as the host to such manufacturers as Colt Industries, Remington, and Winchester-Western. Inexpensive imports not only threatened the profits of the U.S. gun industry, but they also threatened the jobs of ordinary workers in gun factories. Dodd used the hearings to push for new restrictions on mail-order sales of inexpensive imported handguns.

Before any new law could be passed, the assassination of President John F. Kennedy on November 22, 1963, brought the gun-control issue to fever pitch. Kennedy's alleged killer, Lee Harvey Oswald, used a mail-order Italian army surplus rifle. He had seen it advertised in the NRA's *American Rifleman* and ordered it for $19.95 ($21.45 with postage and handling). So Dodd amended his bill to include mail-order rifles and shotguns as well as handguns.

That angered hunters, who pointed out that one effect of the bill would be to raise the prices of the rifles, shotguns, and other weapons used in hunting. So Dodd's bill died. Five years passed without further action on gun control.

Once again, it was an assassination that brought gun-control back to center stage. In April 1968, a bullet from an assassin's rifle killed civil rights leader Martin Luther King Jr. in Memphis, Tennessee. Two months later, another assassin using a pistol killed presidential candidate Robert Kennedy (John Kennedy's brother) in Los Angeles. Congress reacted by passing the Gun Control Act of 1968—the first major gun-control law in thirty years. While some of its prohibitions were eased in 1986, it remains a landmark in firearms legislation.

The Gun Control Act barred interstate mail-order sales of all guns and ammunition—indeed, it forbade almost all interstate gun sales except to dealers. Anyone who made a business of dealing in firearms and ammunition was already required to obtain a federal license. Now, such a dealer would also have to keep detailed records of gun sales. (Among the information to be collected was the buyer's name, race, height, weight, address, and place and date of birth.) The 1968 act prohibited the sale of guns to illegal immigrants and drug addicts, and established extra penalties for anyone who used a gun in committing a federal felony. It also banned the importation of guns that were not "generally recognized as particularly suitable for . . . sporting purposes." It was left up to federal regulators (eventually the Bureau of Alcohol, Tobacco and Firearms) to say what could and could not be imported, and the regulators banned imports of small, cheap handguns and a few types of assault rifles. The law did not stop the importation of *parts* to make such guns, and soon several gun makers in the United States were using imported parts the same types of "Saturday night specials" that had be barred from import. The law also did nothing to stop U.S. gun manufacturers from making cheap handguns with American-made parts. A bill to ban all manufacture of "nonsporting" handguns passed the Senate in 1972 but failed to pass the House.

Rolling Back Gun Control

Passage of the 1968 bill helped to galvanize the NRA into stepped-up efforts to influence federal legislation. During consideration of the 1968 act, a top NRA official had testified before Congress in favor of the bill. But other NRA leaders and many members opposed the bill, seeing *any* type of gun control as a threat to freedom. After an internal struggle that lasted several years, strict opponents of gun control took charge of the NRA in 1977 and have remained in charge ever since.

Backed by powerful grassroots support from its members, the NRA set to work to persuade Congress to roll back gun control. At first its efforts were thwarted by Democratic committee chairmen who supported gun control and used their powers to fend off NRA-backed legislation. Beginning in 1979, Senate hearings explored abuses committed by overzealous agents of the BATF. When the Republicans gained control of the Senate and the White House in 1981, scrutiny of the BATF intensified. For a time, it appeared that the BATF might be abolished. In the end, it was placed on a shorter leash with a smaller budget—a victory for the NRA. The NRA scored another major success with the passage in 1986 of the Firearms Owners Protection Act.

Like most legislation, this act grew out of a series of proposals and counterproposals that were stitched together in endless negotiations and subjected to a series of votes in subcommittees and committees and on the floor of the House and Senate. The process took seven years— from 1979 to 1986. The final bill contained clauses that the NRA strongly opposed, such as a complete ban on the manufacture and sale of machine guns (fully automatic weapons that fire numerous rounds with a single press of the trigger). This ban did contain a "grandfather clause," however, allowing possession of machine guns made before May 19, 1986. The 1986 law also did many things the NRA favored:

- It allowed a resumption of interstate sales of rifles and shotguns, as long as the sales were legal in the states of both seller and buyer.

- It specified that interstate sporting travelers could carry firearms and ammunition while passing through states where such actions are otherwise prohibited, so long as the firearms were not loaded and not directly accessible. (A gun had to be kept in a car trunk, for example, and not in a glove compartment.)

- It eased restrictions on gun dealers: The act allowed gun dealers to sell guns at gun shows. The term "dealer" was defined more narrowly, to make clear that collectors who made occasional sales or exchanges of guns did not need a dealer's license. BATF agents could inspect dealers' records only once each year, unless the agents were making a criminal investigation of someone other than the dealer or were tracing a firearm used in a crime or had first obtained a warrant. Violation of record keeping rules was reduced from a felony charge to a misdemeanor. Record keeping on sales of ammunition was simplified. People who successfully sued to recover guns seized by the BATF were to have their attorneys' fees paid by the government.

- The act required prosecutors in many types of gun-control cases to prove that defendants knew they were breaking a law or regulation.

- It barred the government from creating a national system of firearms registration.

- It toughened penalties for criminal use of firearms.

During debate on the Firearms Owners Protection Act, two other gun-related bills came before Congress. One aimed to ban armor-piercing bullets. The other sought to ban plastic guns that were said to be able to pass undetected through airport screening devices. The proposals pitted the NRA against important segments of the law-enforcement community, since the NRA strongly opposed both bills while many police organizations backed them. The NRA argued that the bills interfered with the choices of hunters and sportspeople. It said the bills would ban many types of ordinary ammunition and many nonplastic guns. It also claimed the bills would open the way for still more gun-control laws, thus whittling away gun owners' constitutional rights. Police organizations argued that law-enforcement officials needed such laws in the fight against crime and terrorism and for protection against "cop-killer" bullets.

Many legislators who normally supported the NRA split with the group on these bills. Some ridiculed the

NRA's stand on armor-piercing bullets, with one senator asking whether deer were wearing armor-plated vests these days. The bullet bill passed and was signed into law in August 1986 after both sides agreed to a compromise that did not ban the most common types of ammunition. The "plastic-gun" ban faced stiffer opposition, with critics of the ban pointing out that such guns were only part plastic and contained metal parts that did in fact show up in airport scans. Debate focused on minimum standards for how much metal a "plastic gun" should contain, with police leaders and gun-control supporters proposing 8.5 ounces (240 grams) of steel. After Vice President George Bush came out for the bill while campaigning in the 1988 New Hampshire presidential primary, it passed Congress with the minimum metal content set at 3.7 ounces (105 grams) of stainless steel. The bill became law in November 1988.

The Brady Bill

By then, a new gun-control proposal was stirring debate. Seven years earlier, on March 30, 1981, two months after Ronald Reagan had started his first term as U.S. president, a deranged gunman named John Hinckley Jr. had fired six shots at Reagan from a .22-caliber revolver as the president left a Washington, D.C., hotel after making a speech. The one bullet that hit Reagan in the chest had done little damage, and Reagan recovered quickly. But Reagan's press secretary, James Brady, was shot just above the left eye and was gravely wounded. The bullet, known as a Devastator because it was designed to explode on impact, splattered dozens of metal fragments into Brady's face and brain. Quick medical treatment saved Brady's life, but he suffered serious brain damage and would never recover the full use of his limbs.

Brady was destined to become a "poster boy" for the gun-control movement. His wife, Sarah Brady, became leader of Handgun Control, Inc., a lobbying group later renamed the Brady Campaign to Prevent Gun Violence. She was an outspoken advocate of a bill to impose a seven-day waiting period on purchases of handguns—a bill dubbed the Brady Bill. She wrote: "The issue is whether the John Hinckleys of the world should be able to walk into gun stores and purchase handguns instantly."[1] First introduced in Congress in 1987, the Brady Bill underwent prolonged debate with fierce opposition from the NRA before

James Brady (left) and others watch President Bill Clinton sign the Brady Bill on January 30, 1993.

finally becoming law in modified form in November 1993.

Under the Brady Handgun Violence Prevention Act (its formal title), those who sought to buy handguns from licensed gun dealers had to wait five (not seven) business days. During that time, local law officers were to conduct a background check. Unless the check found a valid reason for barring the purchase (as would be the case if, for example, the prospective buyer was an illegal alien or had been convicted of a violent felony), the sale could take place at the end of the five-day period. If they found no reason to prevent the sale, law-enforcement agencies had to destroy the buyer's application and keep no record of it. In states that had an alternate method of making background checks, the five-day waiting period did not apply.

Under prodding by the NRA, Congress wrote a "sunset clause" into the Brady Bill, saying that the five-day waiting period would end after five years. During those five years, the Federal Bureau of Investigation (FBI) created a national instant criminal background check system for gun purchases. The Brady Bill's five-day waiting period came to an end in November 1998. Since then, gun dealers have been required to use the national system to make a background check on all sales—not just of handguns but of all guns, with the exception of antiques. The system is designed to let the dealer know immediately if there is any reason the sale cannot go through. Thus, prospective buyers (both "John Does" and "John Hinkleys") no longer have to wait to complete a purchase.

Omnibus Crime Bill

While debate over the Brady Bill was roiling Congress, another gun-control issue came into the picture. It was a

When movie actor Clint Eastwood, in the character of "Dirty Harry" Callahan, told a bad guy to "Make my day," he was urging the guy to go for a gun or otherwise threaten him. Such an action would give Dirty Harry legal justification to shoot to kill.

You can't just shoot someone because he (or she) is breaking the law. For instance, in most states you can't legally shoot a fleeing burglar—even if the culprit has stolen your most precious possession. Nor can you shoot someone trying to break into a car parked on the street. In those cases, your own (or another's) life and safety are not being threatened, and therefore you cannot claim self-defense.

But what if you are in your car when someone tries to break into it? That might make a big difference. Say the assailant takes a hammer and smashes in a window. Will your head be the next target of that hammer? If so, your life is in danger, and you might have valid cause to fire a gun ("use deadly force," in legalese) to protect yourself. Moreover, you are generally allowed to shoot to save the life of some other person.

proposal to ban the sale of assault weapons. Such guns were said to be favored by drug dealers and other criminals, but were also cherished by some collectors, hunters, and sportspersons, and the NRA vigorously opposed most federal restrictions. The issue exploded into national consciousness when a man fired more than one hundred rounds from a Chinese-made AK-47 rifle into a crowded elementary school-yard in Stockton, California, on January 19, 1989. Five children died and thirty other people were wounded.

With many police organizations and mayors calling for a ban on assault guns, several cities (including Stock-

Laws about the use of deadly force are generally state laws, **67** which means that they vary in detail from one location to another. As a rule, however, they follow the same basic principles. Alaska's law is typical. It states that a person is justified in using deadly force if "the person reasonably believes the use of deadly force is necessary for self-defense against death, serious physical injury, kidnapping, sexual assault in the first degree, sexual assault in the second degree, or robbery in any degree." (Note that robbery and burglary are distinctly different crimes. In a robbery, the robber takes something from a person in a direct confrontation under threat of violence. In a burglary, the burglar breaks into a building to steal property.) The Alaska law goes on to state that deadly force is *not* justified "if the person knows that, with complete personal safety and with complete safety as to others, the person can avoid the necessity of using deadly force by retreating." There is an exception, however: Retreat is not necessary if you are attacked in your own home. (Other states have looser or stricter laws on retreat.)

Actually, Harry Callahan was not particularly careful about following the niceties of the law. That's why the maverick cop was called Dirty Harry, after all. (The famous quote above comes from the 1983 movie *Sudden Impact.*)

ton) quickly outlawed the weapons. Many legislatures began considering statewide bans. In March 1989, the Bush administration imposed a temporary ban on imports of AK-47s, Uzis, and several other varieties of assault weapons—a ban that was later extended and made permanent. One result of these actions was a sharp rise in demand for, and production of, U.S.-made assault weapons. With demand soaring, prices rose. Gun factories ran their assembly lines around the clock and still had trouble keeping up with orders.

Years of congressional debate culminated in the adoption of the Omnibus Crime Bill of 1994, which ordered an end to imports and production of semiautomatic weapons with a detachable magazine and more than one assault-weapon feature. Nineteen weapons were banned by name, including the TEC-22 semiautomatic pistol and the Striker 12 revolving-cylinder shotgun. The law also banned U.S. manufacture of ammunition magazines capable of holding more than ten rounds. Under a "grandfather clause," the possession and sale of existing assault weapons and large ammunition clips remained legal. Although a ban to repeal the restrictions on assault weapons passed the Republican-led House in 1996, it did not become law.

The Brady Law does not require background checks for firearms sales by people who are not licensed dealers—for example, private individuals who sell guns to a family member or who make occasional sales at gun shows. In recent years, and especially since the 1999 school shootings in Littleton, Colorado, congressional debate has centered on proposals to extend background checks to such gun-show sales.

Gun Control Pros and Cons

It was Mother's Day in a presidential election year (2000), and tens—maybe hundreds—of thousands of mothers spent it marching for gun control. An event that its sponsors called the Million Mom March drew an enthusiastic crowd to the National Mall in Washington, D.C. There a parade of speakers appealed to Congress to pass a variety of gun-control laws, including registration of all handguns and licensing of handgun owners. Among the marchers was a woman from Ohio, whose college-age son

Participants in the May 2000 "Million Mom March" call for stricter gun laws.

had been fatally shot five years before. She carried a placard that said: "I march today to save a child tomorrow." That same day similar marches were held elsewhere, in cities like Los Angeles and Denver.

The placards and signs bore different messages a few months later when the National Rifle Association held an election rally in Dickson City, Pennsylvania. "8,276,104 semiautomatic guns harmed nobody today," declared one sign. In a speech, NRA president Charlton Heston compared gun-rights supporters to colonial soldiers in the American Revolution, saying: "Instead of fighting the Redcoats, we're fighting the blue-blooded elitists. . . .

Instead of fighting for independence, we are fighting for individual freedom."

When the subject is gun control, tempers quickly rise to fever pitch. Each side has its certainties—its slogans and its arguments. But is anybody on either side listening to what the other side has to say? Sometimes you have to wonder. Each side is capable of presenting cogent arguments for its position. In this chapter, we will present some of those arguments and let readers judge their relative merits.

For Gun Control

Supporters of gun control start with a central conviction—that laws restricting the sale and possession of guns can make life safer for everybody. Two key arguments underlie the case for gun control. The first is that gun-control laws save lives and help to prevent gun-related injuries. The second is that gun-control laws restrict the access of criminals to guns and thereby help to bring crime rates down.

Saving Lives With Gun Control. It's a common item on the evening news: A child picks up a loaded gun and it suddenly goes off, killing the child or a bystander.

- In Florida, two young boys found a shotgun under a bed in their grandparents' home. A six year old pulled the trigger, and a five year old fell dead.

- In Illinois, two teens found a handgun in their grandmother's apartment. The gun went off in the hands of a sixteen-year-old boy, killing his fifteen-year-old cousin.

There was a time when gun-control laws in this country were far-reaching and explicit: No guns, period. (And often no other "weapons"—no knives, no canes, no dogs!) These were not general laws, however, that applied to the public at large. They were laws designed to disarm racial and ethnic minorities. Thus, a Virginia colonial law of 1619 required "free Mulattoes, Negroes and Indians . . . [to] appear without arms."[1] After independence and before the Civil War, most states had laws that restricted the rights of blacks, both free and enslaved, to own or carry arms. After slavery ended, several southern states adopted "race-neutral" gun-control measures—but in practice applied them only to blacks. Native Americans, too, faced special barriers to gun ownership. Not until the twentieth century did the federal government abolish its restrictions on gun sales to Native Americans.

This history of racial and ethnic bias is cited by some commentators today as an argument against gun control. In fact, some authors have seen racism as one of the motivating factors behind existing gun-control laws. Here is what journalist Robert Sherrill had to say in a 1973 book about gun control: "The Gun Control Act of 1968 was passed not to control guns but to control blacks, and inasmuch as a majority of Congress did not want to do the former but were ashamed to show that their goal was the latter, the result was that they did neither."[2] He links the 1968 law to fears about the urban riots that flared during the "long, hot summers" of the 1960s, and to white fear of black militancy in general.

Race does sometimes seem to play a part in how people react to the public display of guns. In Houston, Texas, in June

2000, an organization called the New Black Panther Party staged an armed demonstration outside a state Republican convention. A dozen or so African Americans marched back and forth carrying shotguns and rifles. According to Texas law, it is perfectly legal to carry a gun in a public place—so long as the carrier is not a convicted felon, the gun is at least 26 inches (66 centimeters) long, and the gun is not pointed at anyone or held in a threatening manner. Yet after a convention delegate confronted the demonstrators and was pushed to the ground, a city councilman faulted the police for not stopping the demonstration. The councilman was an opponent of gun control—but somehow felt that the guns in this instance were a special case, in need of control.

Discretionary "concealed-carry" laws are sometimes viewed as a convenient tool for denying equal rights to members of minorities. The concern is that police or other authorities issuing permits for concealed weapons might make biased decisions unfairly denying applications by poor people, blacks, Middle Easterners, people with "foreign" accents, women, gun-rights activists, and advocates of unpopular causes. For that reason, a wide range of organizations from civil-liberties groups to the NRA argue that concealed-carry laws should leave issuing authorities no choice but to grant a permit so long as the applicant meets clearly stated requirements.

Supporters of gun control generally deny that gun control is racist in any way. In fact, they say, gun control benefits racial and ethnic minorities at least as much as it benefits the public at large. They point out that African Americans, especially in urban areas, are more likely than whites to be the victims of gun-associated crimes. By limiting the ability of criminals to get guns, the argument goes, gun control can make life safer for blacks and other minorities.

- In Michigan, a six-year-old boy found a handgun in a shoebox at the house where he was staying with an uncle. He took the gun to school, pulled it out of his pocket, and shot a girl in his first-grade class. She died on the way to the hospital.

Incidents like these happen so often that we've almost come to expect them. But they don't have to happen, say gun-control advocates, if better gun-control laws are passed.

Supporters of gun control find plenty of numbers to bolster their case. For example, they note that firearms take the lives of some 30,000 people in the United States each year. About six hundred of the victims are under age fifteen, and about thirty-five hundred are aged fifteen to nineteen. According to the Centers for Disease Control, a federal agency, firearms take the lives of a far greater proportion of children in the United States than in other industrial nations (Figure 1). A common rule of thumb is that firearms injure about three people for every one they kill.

Note that accidents account for only about a seventh of the deaths caused by firearms. More than half (53 percent) are suicides. Most of the rest (43 percent) are homicides, including both lawful killings (by police or by citizens in self-defense) and unlawful ones. For firearm-related deaths among children, however, homicides exceed suicides.

How could gun-control laws reduce this toll? In many ways, say supporters. For example, a law requiring trigger locks could prevent many accidental shootings by children. So could a law requiring owners to keep guns and ammunition locked up and in separate locations. A three-day or five-day waiting period for gun purchases might

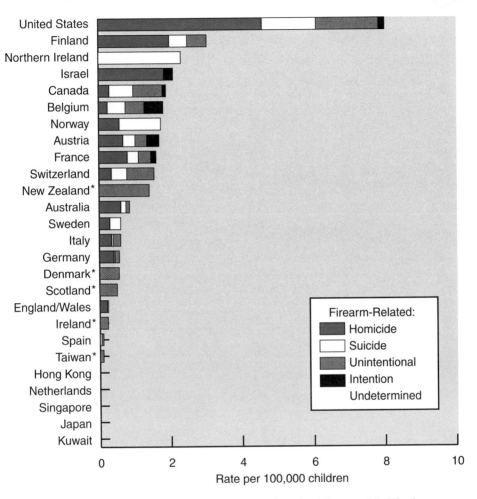

Firearm-Related Deaths Among Children Less Than 15 Years Old in 26 Industrialized Countries For One Year During 1990–1995

Legend — Firearm-Related:
- Homicide
- Suicide
- Unintentional
- Intention
- Undetermined

Rate per 100,000 children

Countries marked by askerisks (*) reported only unintentional firearm-related deaths.
Source: Centers for Disease Control, *Morbidity and Mortality Weekly Report*, February 7, 1997, volume 46 number 5, p. 104

prevent many suicides that occur during a period of deep but temporary depression. A waiting period might also deter people from buying a gun in a fit of anger and using it to shoot someone. And a waiting period would allow authorities to check to see if a gun buyer has a history of mental problems or is subject to a protection-from-abuse order—red flags that are often missed by the federal instant-check system. Another useful gun-control law would be one requiring first-time gun buyers to take a course in gun safety. States that have such laws have found that they help to make gun accidents less likely.

Ads and bumper stickers often express attitudes about gun control.

But one of the most comprehensive proposals for protecting people from guns is to extend U.S. consumer-protection laws to cover firearms. Federal regulation of guns could be patterned after the regulation of such other hazardous products as drugs and pesticides, or such mainstream consumer products as cars and toys. Gun-control advocates point out that federal regulations have forced car makers to incorporate such features as seat belts and air bags, thus making cars far safer than they were in the past. The reason this has not been done with firearms is that the gun industry, backed by gun-rights groups like the NRA, successfully lobbied Congress to bar the Consumer Product Safety Commission from regulating firearms.

To supporters, passing gun-control laws to protect lives is a no-brainer. It should have been done long ago. "If toaster ovens were killing kids in the home, we wouldn't have toaster ovens," said Dr. Jonathan I. Groner, an Ohio surgeon who did a study on gun deaths. "But still there are guns."

From the other side of the gun-control divide, however, things look quite different. Gun-rights supporters question many of the assumptions made in favor of gun control. Take the assumption that a waiting period would increase safety. Gun-rights supporters call waiting periods a "time tax," saying their main effect is to increase the hassle involved in buying a gun. In this view, the waiting period serves to discourage legitimate gun buyers from exercising their right to arm themselves. Someone who is bent on murder will find other ways to acquire a gun—or just use a knife or a rock. Someone who really wants to commit suicide has many other options—an overdose of pills, perhaps, or a razor blade. Yet no one seriously argues that we should ban razor blades to stop suicides. Moreover, a waiting period would stop someone like a stalking victim from quickly acquiring a handgun for self-defense.

Requiring trigger locks also draws the ire of groups like the NRA. It's all well and good, they say, if a gun buyer wants such a device and buys it voluntarily. In fact, the National Shooting Sports Foundation, the trade association of the gun industry, sponsors a program called HomeSafe that hands out free gun locks (worth about $10 each) to as many as one million gun owners a year. A gun-lock giveaway program was started in Texas under former governor George W. Bush, financed by court fees paid by convicted offenders. But why bring big government into the picture by making locks mandatory? Why have the government snoop in private homes to see how guns are stored?

Gun-rights supporters use a similar "big government" argument against the idea of regulating guns as consumer products. Let the market decide, they say. Adding layers of federal regulation will just make guns more expensive to the gun buyer. If gun buyers want guns with particular features, they can buy such guns. But many "safety" features touted by gun-control advocates make guns less safe, or less usable for defense, gun advocates claim. Locks can prevent people from gaining quick access to a gun to fend off an intruder. Gun advocates point to an August 2000 incident in Merced, California, where two children were murdered when a man with a pitchfork burst into their bedrooms. A fourteen-year-old sister might have stopped the man, a family member said, but her father's guns were locked away.

On one point, however, gun-rights and gun-control supporters find common ground. Both agree on the usefulness of gun-safety courses. Since 1988, the NRA has

sponsored "Eddie Eagle" gun-safety courses for use in schools. It also offers hands-on courses for older youths and adults who want to take up shooting sports or who plan to buy a gun for self-defense. All in all, the NRA claims to train more than a million people a year—including police officers—in firearms safety. Many NRA supporters credit the group's courses for the fact that firearms accident rates have declined significantly in the last thirty years—even though there are far more guns in people's possession—and that hunting has one of the lowest accident rates of any outdoor activity.

Reducing Crime With Gun Control. A second line of argument for supporters of gun-control laws is that guns promote crime, and that gun-control laws are needed to bring crime rates down. Many laws already on the books seek to restrict criminals' access to guns. For example, since 1938, federal law has barred the sale of firearms to convicted felons and fugitives.

But gun-control advocates are pushing for much stricter laws. They cite federal studies that seek to trace guns used to commit crimes. In one case, a gun taken from a juvenile arrested in Washington, D.C., was traced to a dealer in St. Louis. After its sale in St. Louis, the gun had passed through the hands of a gun trafficker in Nashville. It was one of two hundred to three hundred guns that the trafficker had sold on the streets of Washington. All told, the study traced 138 crime guns confiscated in Washington back to the same St. Louis dealer. According to the Bureau of Alcohol, Tobacco, and Firearms, 57 percent of guns used in crimes were sold originally by just 1.2 percent of federally licensed dealers. Citing figures such as these, gun-control advocates call for much stricter regulation of dealers.

A second ready source of hard-to-trace guns is private sales at the more than four thousand gun shows held each year in the United States. Gun-control advocates want to "close the gun-show loophole" by extending federal background checks to private gun-show sales. Members of Congress have introduced a number of bills in recent years designed to do that. One was called the McCain–Lieberman Bill after its two main sponsors, Senator John McCain (R-Arizona) and Senator Joe Lieberman (D-Connecticut). Another was called the Reed Bill after its chief sponsor, Senator Jack Reed (D-Rhode Island).

As further crime-control measures, gun-control groups have recently been pushing for such federal measures as these:

Thanks to the Internet, you can easily find a wealth of information about gun laws and gun statistics. Below are some useful links:

The Laws. Information about gun laws can be found at a number of government and issue-group Web sites. For summaries of federal laws:

> Bureau of Alcohol, Tobacco and Firearms
> www.atf.treas.gov/firearms/legal/index.htm

> Brady Campaign to Prevent Gun Violence
> www.bradycampaign.org/legislation/federal/gunlaws.asp

> National Rifle Association
> www.nraila.org/GunLaws.asp

For information about legislation under consideration by the U.S. Congress:

> thomas.loc.gov/

For summaries of state laws:

> Brady Campaign to Prevent Gun Violence
> www.bradycampaign.org/facts/statelaws/index.asp

> National Rifle Association
> www.nraila.org/GunLaws.asp?FormMode=state

Surveys and Statistics. The following sites provide access to surveys, research, and statistics about guns:

> Bureau of Justice Statistics, U.S. Department of Justice
> www.ojp.usdoj.gov/bjs/

> Firearm Injury Center, Medical College of Wisconsin
> www.mcw.edu/fic/

> Injury Mortality Reports, Centers for Disease Control
> www.cdc.gov

> Johns Hopkins Center for Gun Policy and Research
> support.jhsph.edu/departments/gunpolicy/survey.cfm

- Raise the minimum age for possessing a handgun to twenty-one, and also make that the minimum age for possessing an assault weapon.

- Prohibit gun sales to people over eighteen who committed violent crimes before turning eighteen; such people are not covered by the current prohibition on gun sales to felons.

- Extend the 1994 ban on U.S. manufacture of large-capacity ammunition magazines. It is still legal to sell imported ammunition clips and to resell ammunition clips already owned by private individuals. Such sales too should be banned, say gun-control advocates.

Some gun-control supporters want to go much further. They favor the registration of all guns sold and the

Gun Sales

Baloo

"I'm afraid there's a ten day waiting period, but I can sell you a short-term life insurance policy while you're waiting."

licensing of all gun buyers. Note that registration and licensing are distinctly different. Registration is for guns; licensing is for owners.

A national system of *registration* of firearms is prohibited by the Firearm Owners' Protection Act of 1986, thanks to a strong lobbying effort by the NRA. A registry would include a serial number for each gun and a system of tracking sales. If a gun were recovered after a crime, it could presumably be traced back through its previous owners to discover how it came into a criminal's possession. A firearms registry might also include the "ballistic fingerprint" of each gun, as is required for new guns under New York State law. With such a registry, even an ejected shell or a spent bullet at a crime scene might provide enough evidence to identify the gun used.

Licensing of gun buyers would probably work something like the licensing of drivers, which occurs at the state level. In order to purchase a gun, you would have to have a firearms license. Before getting the license, you might have to demonstrate knowledge of the fundamentals of gun safety or take a basic course. According to gun-control supporters, firearms licensing would make it easier to keep guns out of the hands of criminals and would give public authorities additional tools for solving crimes that involve guns. Supporters say protections could be built into the law to prevent its abuse for political or other purposes.

Registration and licensing evoke expressions of horror from gun-rights supporters. Many see such controls as endangering all freedoms, saying they might be used by a tyrannical government to confiscate everyone's guns and crush armed freedom movements. Some gun-rights supporters already compare U.S. gun-control laws to legislation adopted in 1938 by Hitler and the German Nazis.

This legislation, along with earlier gun registration laws, made it easy for the Nazis to confiscate firearms owned by Jews and political opponents. Many gun-rights supporters would agree with NRA leader Wayne LaPierre. In his book *Guns, Crime, and Freedom*, LaPierre refers to the 1938 German law and describes the right to bear arms as "the ultimate safeguard against despotism and genocide."[3]

Except for the measure to bar people with a record of juvenile violence from owning firearms, gun-rights supporters generally reject the other proposals mentioned earlier. They argue that gun dealers already have to comply with extensive regulations—that adding new requirements would lead to new abuses by BATF agents, like the

Pro-gun demonstrators protest Massachusetts's tough gun laws outside the Statehouse in Boston in April 2000.

abuses exposed in congressional inquiries of the 1970s and 1980s. The NRA said it would support an instant background check of no more than twenty-four hours on all guns sold at gun shows. But the organization criticized the McCain–Lieberman Bill as cumbersome, intrusive, and needlessly complex, saying it would be "utterly unworkable" and would make gun shows impossible.

Against Gun Control

Gun-rights supporters have their own vision of the way society should work. In that vision, guns play an important part in bolstering individual freedoms and protecting private citizens from both crime and governmental tyranny. Their position is that guns both save lives and reduce crime. Beyond that, gun-rights supporters argue that gun control is just plain unworkable.

Saving Lives and Property With Guns. One of the most popular features in the NRA-produced *American Rifleman* magazine relates the experiences of gun owners who have used their weapons in self-defense. There's the woman in Washington State who grabbed a handgun and chased a burglar from her bedroom. And the convenience store clerk in Florida who shot a robber in the chest. And the couple in Arkansas who were accosted by two would-be robbers outside their home and exchanged shots with them, killing one. And the group of neighbors in New Mexico who responded to a woman's summons and helped corner a burglar, with one neighbor holding the suspect at gunpoint until police arrived. Gun-rights supporters see such stories as proof of the effectiveness of guns in saving lives and property.

Even gun owners who have never used their guns for self-defense find solace in the fact that the gun is there if needed. As NRA research director Paul Blackman told ABC News: "There is a potent psychological benefit in having a gun—like [having] iron bars or an alarm system."[4]

There are also stories about what happens when people don't have guns when they need them. In October 1991, an angry man crashed his pickup into a cafeteria in Killeen, Texas, jumped out of the truck, and opened fire with two semiautomatic pistols. He killed twenty-two people and wounded twenty in the worst gun massacre in U.S. history. Suzanna Gratia managed to crawl to safety but lost both her parents in the massacre. She was heartbroken that she had not been carrying her gun in her purse that day. If someone in the cafeteria had had a gun, she told a TV reporter, the massacre might have been stopped. (Some years later, Ms. Gratia—now Dr. Gratia-Hupp—was elected to the Texas state legislature as a strong advocate of gun rights.)

From the gun-control side, such stories seem less than convincing. Supporters of gun control cite other stories about guns intended for self-defense—stories about assailants grabbing guns from gun owners' hands and using them against the owner, or about gun owners who awake in the night and shoot a family member they mistake for a burglar. Supporters of gun control also argue that gun owners themselves contribute unwittingly to the flow of guns to criminals. In one recent year, more than 600,000 guns were reported stolen from some 250,000 U.S. households. That's 600,000 more guns in the hands of the bad guys.

Interpreting statistics about the success of using guns in self-defense is not always easy. Serious researchers sometimes disagree about the meaning of a particular set of data. According to Gary Kleck, a professor of criminology at Florida State University, there are about as many defensive uses of guns by citizens each year as there are criminal uses of guns. But another researcher, David Hemenway, calls Kleck's figures for defensive gun use "extreme overestimates."

Contrary to a common opinion, Kleck argues, people who wield guns in self-defense against robberies and assaults are less likely to be injured than are victims who do not resist. They are also less likely to lose their money or their valuables. Citing interviews with people in prison, Kleck says that criminals who think a potential victim has a gun will often pick another victim instead, meaning that gun possession can serve as a protection against crime. Guns, summarizes Kleck, "are a source of both social order and disorder, depending on who uses them. . . ."[5]

Supporters of gun rights argue that the best way to attack crime is to establish stiff laws against the use of guns in crime and to strictly enforce those laws. "I think we've got enough laws on the books [about guns]," said John Ashcroft, U.S. attorney general in the administration of President George W. Bush. "I think what we need is tougher enforcement." A related thought is expressed by a bumper sticker: "GUN CONTROL ISN'T CRIME CONTROL."

"Gun Control Doesn't Work." Which brings us to another key argument of the gun-rights movement—that no matter how many gun-control laws are passed, criminals will still get guns and use them against the public. Drug dealers won't apply for gun licenses and they won't go to gun stores and buy registered guns—they'll steal any guns they need or buy them from crooks. The same for bank robbers and rapists. Only law-abiding citizens will obey gun laws, and if those laws discourage gun ownership, then criminals will gain an edge over the rest of us. In the words of journalist J. Neil Schulman: "The decent people need to be better armed than the criminals, or the criminals will win."[6] A bumper-sticker slogan sums it up: "IF GUNS ARE OUTLAWED, ONLY OUTLAWS WILL HAVE GUNS."

To which many supporters of gun control respond that they do not want to *ban* all guns. They say the object of gun-control laws is much more limited—to make firearms safer, to reduce the carnage caused by the misuse of guns, and to keep guns out of dangerous hands. Some gun-control supporters go further and propose banning all handguns, and even some long guns, but not all guns.

But gun-rights supporters express outrage at the idea that guns are a problem in the first place. In the words of a popular slogan: "GUNS DON'T KILL PEOPLE—PEOPLE DO." Which is why the gun-rights movement is so insistent on tougher law enforcement. Put the bad guys in jail, the argument goes, and the rest of us can go about our business—and yes, we'll keep our guns, thank you, since some of the bad guys are still on the loose.

A Terrorist Connection?

Terrorism and efforts to control it play a part in the gun debate. After terrorists hijacked four planes and crashed three of them into buildings in New York and Virginia on September 11, 2001, killing thousands, fear of other terrorist acts spread widely. Gun sales increased as more people bought guns for self-defense. A gun-rights group in California put up billboards urging the passage of laws to make it easier to have a gun in the home or on the person. "Society is safer," the billboards said, "when criminals don't know who's armed."[7]

Congress gave quick passage to a series of laws requested by President George W. Bush to expand the powers of authorities to investigate and prevent terrorist activities. Both sides in the gun debate entered the fray. The NRA voiced support for a strengthening of antiterrorist laws, including the arming of airline pilots, but cautioned against any infringements on individual rights. Sarah Brady, the head of the Brady Campaign to Prevent Gun Violence, also supported the antiterrorist legislation. However, she called for further steps to "close the gaps in our federal firearm laws that allow terrorists to amass their deadly arsenals." Linking background checks on private sales at gun shows to the fight against terrorism, she added: "We must . . . ensure that there are records of all firearm sales so that law enforcement officials can track terrorists [and] trace their weapons. . . ."[8]

Gun-control advocates have claimed that terrorists or their supporters were buying weapons at U.S. gun shows and shipping them to terrorists overseas. They cited the conviction one day before the horrific attacks of September 11, 2001, of a Lebanese man and his brother in Michigan. They were accused of buying shotguns, ammunition, assault weapon parts, and other items with the intent of shipping them to anti-Israeli militants in Lebanon. The NRA said the convictions proved that existing laws work when they are enforced. "Passing gun show restrictions will in no way deter such a committed criminal," the NRA declared. "That can only be done by aggressive law enforcement action, like we saw in this case."[9]

Legislation on the Table

Both sides of the gun debate have been campaigning for new laws at the federal level. On the gun-control side, the big push in recent years has been to "close the gun-show loophole." That is the aim of the McCain–Lieberman and Reed bills discussed earlier, and of other measures as well. Another major proposal is to require licensing of handgun purchasers. On the gun rights side, attention has focused on efforts to make it harder for cities and states to sue gun makers. During the 1990s, about two dozen such suits were filed, accusing gun companies of selling flawed products (too few safety features) and selling them in ways that made it too easy for criminals and juveniles to buy them. At the urging of gun-rights lobbyists, a number of states passed "reckless lawsuit preemption" laws barring the state or municipalities from filing such suits. A federal law could achieve the same ends more effectively, banning suits by all states as well as all cities.

CHAPTER 6

"To Keep and Bear Arms"

In the predawn darkness sixteen-year-old William Diamond beat a *rat-tat-tat* on his drum, calling the men of Lexington, Massachusetts, to the town center. The men came with their guns ready. They were Lexington's "minutemen," ready at a moment's notice to take up arms in defense of their homes and families.

It was April 19, 1775, and the town of Lexington was abuzz. Around midnight, Paul Revere had arrived on horseback from Boston with the news that British soldiers were on the march. Their goal was to confiscate arms

This engraving entitled *The Struggle at Concord Bridge* by W. J. Edwards shows the Revolutionary War militia fending off the British.

that colonists had stored at nearby Concord, and to arrest patriot leaders John Hancock and Samuel Adams, who were hiding in Lexington. Revere's warning allowed Hancock and Adams to slip away and gave the minutemen time to assemble. When the redcoats arrived at dawn, some seventy men were at the town center with their guns loaded, but under instructions to hold their fire. From an unknown location, a shot suddenly rang out. The British troops replied with a volley of fire. The War of American

Independence had begun—touched off by "the shot heard 'round the world."

The minutemen who faced the British at Lexington (and later that same day at Concord) were members of local militias—armed citizens organized for self-defense. About 70 percent of the soldiers who fought on the American side in the War of Independence were militiamen, not soldiers in the regular army. After independence had been won, militias remained an important arm of American defense. They are mentioned in the Constitution and in the Bill of Rights (Second Amendment). And they are deeply entangled in present-day disputes over the right to bear arms and the legitimacy of gun-control laws.

Importance of Militias

Militias played a far more important role in colonial America than they did elsewhere. In Europe, rulers tended to distrust "the people" and tried to prevent them from arming themselves. European rulers generally depended on professional armies both to fight wars against outside enemies and to put down uprisings among their own subjects. England did have militias, but it also had laws about who could and could not bear arms. At various times England denied the right to bear arms to the lower classes, to Jews, to Protestants, and to Catholics.

Control of the militia was an important element of a ruler's power. On the eve of the English Civil War of the 1640s, Parliament claimed the right to control the militia—to which King Charles I responded, "By God, not for an hour!"[1] In 1688, after a further period of turbulence and religious quarrels, the English Parliament invited William and Mary to take the throne, but required them to agree to an English Bill of Rights that (among other things) guaranteed a right to bear arms. But the right was limited. It said: "The subjects which are Protestants may have arms for their defence suitable to their conditions and allowed by law."[2] In other words, the right applied only to Protestants and was qualified by a person's social standing ("condition")—a weapon that was suitable for a member of the upper class was not necessarily suitable for a person of lower standing. Moreover, laws could put further restrictions on the right to bear arms, such as restrictions on hunting by commoners.

In the British colonies of North America, where professional soldiers were expensive to maintain, militias were considered essential to colonial defense. They were formed by local communities. Militia members elected their own officers, often subject to approval by their colony's legislature. At times, all the adult males in a community were required by law to have their own firearms and join the militia. A militia mustered (assembled) every few months or perhaps once a year for drill. The rest of the time, militia members pursued their civilian occupations, unless called out for service in an emergency. Because of their haphazard organization and limited training, militias were scorned by officers of regular armies—often with justification. At the same time, militias were feared for their troublemaking potential—say, in stirring up an unwanted war with Native Americans or in threatening armed opposition to a colonial governor.

The Constitution adopted by the United States in 1789 recognized the existence of militias and considered them to be essentially under state control. For example, it was up to the states to appoint officers and provide training for the militias. However, the Constitution gave to Congress the power to prescribe the rules ("discipline") under which the militias were to operate. And Congress had the power to call up state militias to enforce national laws, put down rebellions, and repel invasions. Moreover, the Constitution reserved to the national government the power to make war and to maintain a regular army ("keep Troops").

The Second Amendment

The Bill of Rights was added in response to complaints that the 1789 Constitution lacked a mechanism for protecting individual freedoms. Ratified by the states in 1791, the Bill of Rights consisted of ten amendments. The one that interests us here is the Second Amendment, which guaranteed "the right of the people to keep and bear Arms." But those ten words are only a part of the Second Amendment, and the phrasing of the full amendment (see sidebar on page 96) has given rise to clashing interpretations and bitter controversy.

In essence, the quarrel comes down to this: Is the right to bear arms a *collective* right, closely linked to the right of states to maintain militias, or is it an *individual* right, guaranteed to all Americans whether or not they are members of militias? In the current national debate over gun control, supporters of gun control tend to play down the Second Amendment, interpreting it as relevant only to the question of militias. Supporters of gun rights, on the contrary, tend to see the Second Amendment as a sweeping guarantee of an individual's right to own and use firearms.

Before the twentieth century, the Second Amendment had little impact. It was rarely mentioned in political debate or in court decisions. In one of the few court cases that did mention the Second Amendment, the U.S.

Article I, Section 8 [powers of Congress]
. . . To provide for calling forth the Militia to execute the Laws of the Union, suppress Insurrections and repel Invasions;

To provide for organizing, arming, and disciplining the Militia, and for governing such Part of them as may be employed in the Service of the United States, reserving to the States respectively, the Appointment of the Officers, and the Authority of training the Militia according to the discipline prescribed by Congress. . . .

Article I, Section 10 [powers prohibited to states]
. . . No State shall, without the Consent of Congress, . . . keep Troops, or Ships of War in time of Peace, enter into any Agreement or Compact with another State, or with a foreign Power, or engage in War, unless actually invaded, or in such imminent Danger as will not admit of delay.

Bill of Rights: Second Amendment
A well regulated Militia, being necessary to the security of a free State, the right of the people to keep and bear Arms, shall not be infringed.

Supreme Court ruled in 1875 that the amendment restricted actions of the federal government only—it did not prevent private individuals or states from interfering with the right to bear arms. (The 1875 case, *United States* v. *Cruikshank*, began when armed whites—apparently members of the Ku Klux Klan—were charged with disarming a group of African Americans during an election dispute in Louisiana. This action was said to have deprived the

African Americans of various rights, including the right to bear arms. The Supreme Court overturned the whites' convictions.)

In 1886 the Supreme Court reaffirmed its position that the Second Amendment does not bind state governments. In *Presser* v. *Illinois*, the Court upheld the conviction of a leader of a German-American society that conducted armed military drills without a required state license. However, the Court also said that citizens have an individual right to bear certain types of arms—specifically, arms suitable for use by militias that might be called upon to support the national government.

After Congress passed the first federal gun-control law, the Firearms in the Mails Act, in 1927, the Second Amendment became part of the debate over gun control. And in 1939 the Supreme Court issued a ruling that stands today as its only major pronouncement on the Second Amendment. The Court's ruling upheld the National Firearms Act of 1934 and its regulation of sawed-off shotguns and fully automatic weapons—but it left many other issues unsettled.

The 1939 case revolved around the actions of two suspected bootleggers, Jack Miller and Frank Layton. They were accused of illegally taking an unregistered sawed-off shotgun from Oklahoma to Arkansas (across state lines, and thus "in interstate commerce"). They were also charged with failing to pay a $200 tax imposed by the 1934 law. A district court in Arkansas threw out the case, saying the National Firearms Act violated the men's Second Amendment right to bear arms. The two men were freed, and promptly dropped out of sight, leaving no forwarding address. When the federal government appealed the case, there was no lawyer to argue on behalf of the defendants, so the Supreme Court heard only the government's side.

In its ruling (*United States v. Miller*), the Supreme Court upheld the 1934 law and overturned the lower court's decision. The Court declared that the term "militia," as used in the Constitution, meant "all males physically capable of acting in concert for the common defense"[3]—that is, almost the entire male population. At the time the Constitution and Bill of Rights were adopted, men were expected to appear for service "bearing arms supplied by themselves and of the kind in common use at the time." But the Court declared that it could see no "reasonable relation" between "a shotgun having a barrel of less than eighteen inches in length" and "the preservation or efficiency of a well regulated militia." Therefore, said the Court, it "cannot say that the Second Amendment guarantees the right to keep and bear such an instrument."[4]

In recent years that ruling has been subjected to many and varied readings. Both sides in the gun-control debate have interpreted the ruling in the best possible light for their own position. Many supporters of gun control see it as a definitive statement that the right to bear arms is subordinate to the right of the states to maintain militias (or, since 1903, the National Guard). They see *United States v. Miller* as leaving the way open to a wide range of gun-control laws, perhaps even extending as far as a ban on private ownership of firearms. In contrast, advocates of gun rights interpret the ruling to mean that the Second Amendment protects a person's right to own any gun of military usefulness. (They dispute, by the way, the idea that a shotgun of less than 18 inches (46 centimeters) is not a military weapon, noting that some cavalry units have, in fact, carried short-barreled shotguns.) Also, gun-rights supporters say the Court might have decided differently if it had heard arguments on both sides of the case. Until and unless the Court takes on another Second Amendment case, the dueling interpretations will keep the issue alive.

Interpreting the Second Amendment

"The right of the people to keep and bear Arms shall not be infringed." Those words from the Second Amendment are emblazoned across the main Web page of the National Rifle Association (www.mynra.com). They show the importance that the NRA attaches to the Second Amendment. And they highlight the part of the amendment that the NRA and gun-rights supporters in general tend to stress. But critics of the NRA's position point out that those fourteen words are only part of the Second Amendment. They leave out the opening thirteen words—"A well regulated Militia, being necessary to the security of a free State." And those words are the portion of the Second Amendment that gun-control advocates tend to stress.

At times it seems that everyone has an opinion—often expressed in tones of adamant certainty—about what the Second Amendment means. Politicians expound upon it in campaign speeches. Citizens pour out their feelings about it in letters to the editor. Talk-show impresarios rail about its importance or its insignificance. Scholars dissect its language and probe its meanings in lengthy articles laced with footnotes. Judges cite it in their rulings. Yet for all the bombast and all the scholarship, consensus eludes us.

The debate over the Second Amendment tends to focus on a few key elements. What was the English background of the right to bear arms? What did our nation's Founders have to say about gun rights? How were the exact words of the Second Amendment decided upon? Was the amendment intended to declare a new right, or was it simply reaffirming a right that was part of English common law?

Throughout English history up to 1689, gun control was a fact of life. Sometimes gun control was applied negatively, denying gun rights to certain groups on grounds of religion or class or political activity. At other times gun control was applied positively, requiring people of certain classes to possess arms and employ them when needed in the service of the state, as part of a militia. (Until after the mid-1600s, England had no standing army.) In this positive sense of gun control, bearing arms was more a duty than a right. The turbulent 1600s convinced many English leaders that widespread ownership of firearms was a necessary check on the tyrannical tendencies of rulers. After two successive kings had sought to restrict gun ownership by Protestants while arming the kings' mainly Roman Catholic supporters, the English revolted. The English Bill of Rights of 1689 reflects this history, guaranteeing the right of Protestants to bear arms (with the conditions discussed above). This right was understood as enhancing the ability of people to defend themselves against the government if it became oppressive.

(Not that the English Bill of Rights put an end to gun control in the British Isles. Regulations on guns continued in effect, although they were applied rather lightly for the next few centuries. Since the 1920s, however, as we shall see in the next chapter, Britain has enacted a series of gun-control laws that place sweeping restrictions on the purchase and use of many kinds of firearms.)

The Founders of our own nation were deeply influenced by the English Bill of Rights. They themselves had participated in a revolution that depended on an armed public to help overthrow a government deemed to be oppressive. This experience lay behind their appreciation of militias and their support for the widespread possession of firearms. But did they also believe that governments should leave firearms completely free of control or regulation, as some readings of the Second Amendment imply? That question has received conflicting answers in the current national debate.

Gun-rights supporters cite many statements by the Founders that they interpret as supporting an unconditional right to bear arms. For example, Patrick Henry said: "The great object is that every man be armed. . . . Everyone who is able may have a gun."[5] And gun-rights supporters note that James Madison, who is considered the main author of the Bill of Rights, began his original draft of the Second Amendment with the "right of the people to keep and bear arms,"[6] positioning those words before a reference to "a well armed and well regulated militia." (This order was reversed during consideration by Congress.)

But gun-control supporters are equally adept at finding quotes. They note that Madison's original proposal for the Second Amendment ended with the words "but no person religiously scrupulous of bearing arms [that is, who has a religious objection to bearing arms] shall be compelled to render military service in person,"[7] and they conclude from this that "bear arms" in the Second Amendment has an exclusively military meaning.

The Second Amendment evolved through a number of drafts, undergoing a series of changes along the way. For example, the clause about religious scruples was

U.S. courts have a long history of interpreting the Second Amendment and laws that control the possession and use of firearms. Here are some notable cases:

Dred Scott v. *Sandford,* **1857.** In its controversial decision upholding slavery, the pre–Civil War Supreme Court held that Dred Scott, a slave, was not a U.S. citizen—and that no person of African descent whose ancestors were slaves could be a citizen. Without specifically mentioning the Second Amendment, the Court stated that if "persons of the Negro race" should be recognized as citizens, then they could not be denied the full rights of citizens, including the right "to keep and carry arms wherever they went."

United States v. *Cruikshank,* **1875.** The Supreme Court held that the Second Amendment does not prevent private individuals or states from interfering with the right to bear arms.

Presser v. *Illinois,* **1886.** The Supreme Court upheld a state law that barred armed private groups from parading or drilling in public without a license.

Cases v. *United States,* **1942.** The Court of Appeals for the First Circuit upheld the Federal Firearms Act of 1938 and its ban on gun possession by a convicted felon. The gun in question was a pistol in the possession of a man named José Cases Velázquez. The court said the federal government had the power to regulate the bearing of arms but could not place an outright ban on any weapon useful to a militia. It also said there was no evidence that Cases intended to use the pistol for military purposes.

United States **v.** *Warin,* **1976.** The Court of Appeals for the Sixth Circuit upheld the conviction of a gun designer for possessing a military-style machine gun in violation of federal law. It said the federal government could regulate the ownership and use of firearms. It also said that the Second Amendment established a collective and not an individual right to bear arms.

Quilici **v.** *Village of Morton Grove,* **1982.** The Court of Appeals for the Seventh Circuit upheld a ban placed on handguns by the village of Morton Grove, Illinois. It stated that the Second Amendment does not apply to state and local governments, and that the ban did not conflict with the Illinois constitution.

United States **v.** *Lopez,* **1995.** The Gun-Free School Zones Act of 1990 barred the possession of firearms in or near schools. A twelfth-grade student named Lopez was convicted of violating the law by taking a concealed handgun into his school in Texas. (A state charge of possessing a firearm on school premises had been dropped when the federal charge was filed.) The U.S. Supreme Court overturned the conviction, saying Congress lacked the power to regulate schools. The Court said the 1990 act did not address an economic issue and thus was not a valid application of Congress's power to regulate interstate commerce. (Congress had already found a way around the ruling by passing the Gun-Free Schools Act of 1994. This law used the lure of federal funds, saying that states wishing to receive federal funding would have to make rules to expel students who bring firearms to school. The new law led to widespread adoption of a zero-tolerance policy on weapons of any kind in schools.)

Printz **v.** *United States,* **1997.** The Supreme Court threw out a part of the Brady Law that required state officials to participate in background checks of people seeking to buy handguns within their state. The Court held that this was a violation of states' rights. Other parts of the Brady Act were unaffected.

dropped. And the Senate voted down a proposed amendment that would have qualified the right to keep and bear arms with the additional words "for the common defense." Supporters of gun rights argue that the defeat of this amendment means the Founders considered the right to bear arms to be an individual rather than a collective right.

During the early and mid-1990s, a number of scholarly studies supported the idea that the Second Amendment was intended to establish an *individual* right to bear arms. Citing extensive research in historical sources, writers like Joyce Lee Malcolm and Glenn Harlan Reynolds took this position. Scholars also concluded that a large proportion of early Americans owned and used guns. A consensus seemed to be forming among historians and scholars of the Constitution that, at least in the minds of the Founders, the right to keep and bear arms belonged to all people, whether or not they were active in militias.

More recently, however, rival scholars have challenged those conclusions, citing other research findings. For example, Lois G. Schwoerer and Jack N. Rakove put forth alternative interpretations of English history and the U.S. constitutional debates. Rakove claimed that the debate over the Second Amendment was mainly about states' rights, not individual ownership of firearms. Another scholar, Michael Bellesiles, made an extensive study of legal records, such as wills in which people list the property they are passing on to their heirs. He concluded that before 1850 only about 10 percent of the population (and perhaps a third of white males) owned guns. (Bellesiles's findings were challenged by gun-rights advocates and historians who rechecked his work and found serious errors. The author made some revisions for a paperback edition, but defended his theory.)

While the debate usually focuses on federal gun rights, supporters of gun rights point out that forty-four state constitutions contain provisions that recognize a right to bear arms. Some of these date from the American Revolution; others have been added in recent times. In 1998 when it amended its constitution, Wisconsin became the forty-fourth state to include such a provision. Its charter says: "The people have the right to keep and bear arms for security, defense, hunting, recreation or any other lawful purpose."[8] (Article 1, section 25)

Many state constitutions declare explicitly that the right to own and possess guns is an individual right. For example, Alaska's constitution states: "The individual right to keep and bear arms shall not be denied or infringed by the State or a political subdivision of the State."[9] (Article 1, section 19) In Alaska and often elsewhere, the right to bear arms is linked to a right to self-defense. Such rights are not necessarily regarded as unlimited, however. State courts have held many kinds of gun regulations to be consistent with an individual right to bear arms.

Perhaps it is too much to hope that some future Supreme Court decision can settle the debate. Many other constitutional issues have remained in dispute even after what seemed to be clear Supreme Court rulings. There are always side issues or unforeseen circumstances that come along to muddy the water. Then again, the high court's rulings often provide definitive answers to one set of questions and thus serve to refocus public debate, perhaps giving rise to new sets of related questions.

One prominent Second Amendment case was moving through the courts early in the twenty-first century. It involved a Texas doctor named Timothy Joe Emerson who got in trouble for having a gun. Like many men going through a contested divorce, Emerson had been placed under a standard court order (called a restraining order) not to harass or threaten his wife. The wife, Sasha Emerson, had claimed that Emerson threatened a man she had been dating. Under the Violence Against Women Act of 1994, the restraining order meant that Emerson was barred from possessing a firearm—although neither he nor the judge issuing the order seems to have been aware of that point.

One day Sasha Emerson stopped by Emerson's medical office in San Angelo, Texas. There, she claimed, Emerson threatened her, showing a gun in the presence of their six-year-old daughter. Emerson said it wasn't so—and was eventually acquitted on charges involving the incident. Nonetheless, accused of violating the Violence Against Women Act by possessing a firearm, he was hauled into federal district court. His lawyer argued that Emerson had no history of violent acts and that no evidence had been presented in support of his wife's earlier claim that he had threatened her friend. The lawyer argued that Emerson's right to due process had been violated when he was denied possession of firearms. Moreover, the lawyer argued that under the Second Amendment, Emerson had a constitutional right to keep a firearm.

In April 1999, Federal District Judge Sam R. Cummings dismissed the charge against Emerson, stating that "a textual analysis of the Second Amendment supports an individual right to bear arms." He said it was not right that a routine restraining order could have the effect of

taking away a right of such importance, adding, "There
must be a limit to government regulation on lawful
firearm possession."[10]

The U.S. government appealed the decision. More
than fifty groups representing many shades of opinion
offered their views to the New Orleans–based U.S. Court
of Appeals for the Fifth Circuit. In October 2001, the
appeals court ruled that the Second Amendment did
indeed give individuals a right to own firearms—the first
such ruling by a high-level court in recent times. "We hold
. . . that [the Second Amendment] protects the right of
individuals, including those not . . . actually a member of
any militia or engaged in active military service or training, to privately possess and bear their own firearms . . .
that are suitable as personal, individual weapons . . . ," the
court declared.[11] However, the court said the Constitution
did not rule out a law aimed at protecting someone from
being threatened with a gun. It said its ruling "does not
mean that [Second Amendment] rights may never be
made subject to any limited, narrowly tailored specific
exceptions or restrictions." The judges sent the case back
to Texas for a new trial, saying that restrictions on Emerson's gun ownership were to continue in the meantime.

While the appeals court's decision was binding only in
three southern states, its interpretation of the Second
Amendment became part of the debate over gun rights
and gun control. An NRA lobbyist observed: "We'll obvi-
ously look for other cases to make the same point, using
this case as a precedent."[12] Gun-control organizations
took heart from the court's finding that lawmakers can
indeed put restrictions on gun ownership and possession.
And so the debate went on. We can expect it to continue
for many years to come.

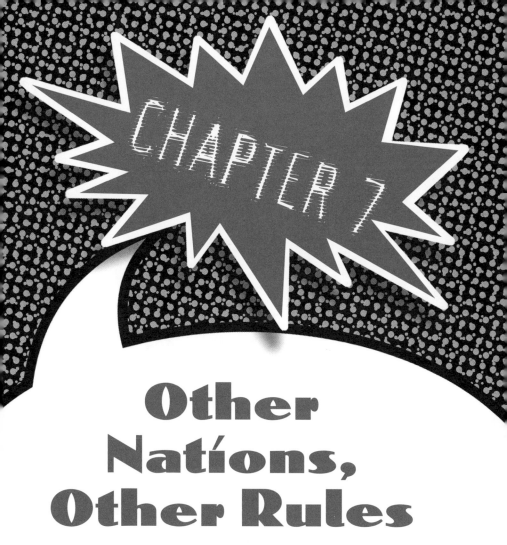

CHAPTER 7

Other Nations, Other Rules

In much of the world, the United States has a reputation as a land of wild-eyed gunslingers. Murder rates in the United States are far higher than those of most other industrial nations. The statistics on murders by handgun are dramatic: In 1996 handgun murders totaled 2 in New Zealand, 15 in Japan, 30 in Great Britain, and 106 in Canada. In the United States that same year, handguns were used to kill 9,390 people.[1] Even taking into account the smaller populations of the other nations, the United States stands out.

Police in many European countries carry billy clubs rather than guns. Here British police learn to use martial arts in dealing with violent criminals.

We see a similar story when we look at murder rates per 100,000 people per year. (These include murders using weapons other than firearms.) The rate in the United States has been dropping lately, but it typically ranges from 6 to 10 per 100,000 people per year. Comparable rates are about 0.5 in Japan, 1.1 in France, 1.3 in England, and 3.4 in Germany.

Are these figures relevant to the debate over gun control? The answer you get depends on whom you ask. For gun-control supporters, the figures are quite relevant. Most of the nations mentioned have much stricter gun-control laws than the United States does, and so the gun-control side sees the murder figures as evidence that gun control can make a difference—a big difference. But gun-rights supporters say the figures have little relation to gun control. They argue that cultural differences among nations account for most of the differences in murder figures. And they cite statistics to argue that in some cases, crime rates have gone *up* after other nations tightened gun controls.

Certainly cultural factors can be important. Just watch the children in a Japanese classroom quietly following the teacher's instructions. You realize at once that you are not in a U.S. classroom, where children are far more likely to be distracting one another or challenging the teacher's instructions. The Japanese people have learned through centuries of tradition to conform quietly to social standards and to accept authority. They are unlikely to jaywalk or to confront a police officer in a challenging manner. They are less likely than Americans to break the law—and when they do, they face a police force with sweeping powers to investigate and interrogate them before bringing them to justice. It seems likely that a significant part of the difference between Japanese and U.S. murder rates is linked to such influences.

Cultural factors also come into play in people's decisions about whether to own guns. In the United States, with its raw colonial background and frontier traditions, gun ownership has been spread over almost all classes and regions. About three hundred Americans in every one thousand own guns. In contrast, in many other countries gun ownership is quite rare. In the European nation of the Netherlands, for instance, only about nine people in one thousand own guns. In Japan, too, few people own or use guns, due to strict gun-control laws and cultural differences.

As this discussion indicates, gun-control laws are only one part of a complex mix of influences. For example, neither Great Britain nor the United States had much in the way of gun control prior to the twentieth century, and yet murder rates were far higher in the United States even then. Nonetheless, it can be instructive to take a closer look at a few selected nations and their approaches to guns and gun control.

Switzerland

The tiny nation of Switzerland in the center of Europe has low crime rates plus a relatively high rate of gun ownership.

With a tradition of neutrality and national self-reliance, Switzerland has what amounts to a national militia in which all male citizens are expected to serve. Young men undergo military training and then serve in the militia-style army until the age of forty-two, doing active duty for two or three weeks each year.

If you were a Swiss burglar, you would do well to avoid breaking into homes in which any of the occupants are adult males. You might be met by an armed householder, because a large proportion of Swiss men keep guns. During a man's period of military service, he is issued a fully automatic assault rifle and ammunition that he is required to keep at home. After leaving the army, Swiss men generally keep their weapon and continue to practice shooting skills.

But Switzerland is not an "anything goes" society. It has long had gun-control laws at the regional level. (Switzerland is divided into regions called cantons, which are roughly equivalent to our states.) After a series of multiple gun murders, the voters in 1993 approved a constitutional amendment allowing the national government to adopt gun controls. Under a Swiss law passed in 1997, people who want to purchase guns in Switzerland must now get a permit from the government of the canton in which they live. Permits are denied to people who have committed violent crimes or who are believed to represent a risk to others. Also, permit holders must be above the age of eighteen.

Even those who possess a gun permit cannot just take a gun wherever they want. In order to bear arms in public, people must apply for a special certificate and show why they need to carry a gun. They must also pass an examination testing their knowledge of gun safety and of Swiss gun laws. Such permits are valid for five years.

Britain

Britain had neither gun controls nor much gun crime during the nineteenth century. In the aftermath of World War I, however, with the triumph of a Communist revolution in Russia and social unrest in much of Europe, the British government began to fear a workers' revolution. Amid publicity about a supposed postwar crime wave, Parliament passed the Firearms Act of 1920 requiring owners of handguns and rifles to be licensed. Further gun controls (licensing of shotgun ownership) came in 1967.

Pressure to pass still more gun-control laws followed sensational mass murders at Hungerford, England, in 1987 and at Dunblane, Scotland, in 1996. At Hungerford, a man stalked through the streets with a semiautomatic rifle, shooting anyone he saw, killing sixteen people (including his own mother) before taking his own life. At Dunblane, a man used a semiautomatic pistol to kill sixteen kindergarten pupils and their teacher in a primary school gym. Then he, too, committed suicide. Stunned by these rare outbursts of gun violence, some Britons called for a complete ban on the private ownership of guns. This did not happen, although the government further tightened existing gun controls and, in 1997, banned handguns.

Under current British law, certain other types of firearms (for example, machine guns and most self-loading shotguns and rifles) are also outlawed. They can be acquired only with the authorization of a high government official and are almost never permitted to private individuals. To buy or keep other rifles and shotguns, people must apply for a license, and police authorities must agree that they have a good reason for keeping a gun. Hunting and recreational shooting are generally considered valid reasons; self-protection is not.

Japan

Japan is said to have the most restrictive firearms regulations in the world. The basic rule is that all firearms are prohibited—except where the law sets out an exception. Thus, in a country of about 126 million people, there are only about a half million firearms, and almost all of those are shotguns.

You can get a gun license in Japan if you fit into an approved category—for example, certain kinds of government officials, licensed hunters, target shooters, and athletes competing in shooting sports. Licensed gun dealers can also possess guns, as can collectors of antique weapons. Regulations carefully specify the way weapons must be stored. They are to be kept out of sight in a locked cabinet, unloaded and partially disassembled, with a chain running through the trigger guard. Gun owners must supply police with a map of their homes showing where the cabinet is located. And ammunition must be kept under lock and key—in a separate location.

To get a license to keep a gun, the Japanese must fill out a series of forms, produce a medical certificate, attend a course on gun safety, and demonstrate knowledge about firearms and skill at using them. The police can turn down an applicant who belongs to, or is believed to associate with, a suspect political group. After three years, the gun license expires—and the person must go through the process again. Each year the person's gun must be inspected to verify that it is not being misused. And if the gun should happen to be stolen and used in a crime, the gun owner may be subjected to severe penalties—almost as if the owner had been the one who committed the crime.

Israel

The threat of terrorism has kept Israeli society on edge for years. Many Israeli civilians carry guns for use in case of a terrorist attack—but stringent laws govern who can carry guns and under what circumstances.

Like Switzerland, Israel has compulsory military service. While Switzerland requires only men to serve, Israel drafts women as well. After completing their service, Israeli men (but not women) must remain in the military reserve and do one month a year of reserve duty until the age of forty-five. While on reserve duty, they must carry their weapons—even during home leave.

Also likely to be armed are Israeli civilians who live or work in majority-Palestinian territories, such as the West Bank, that are under Israeli occupation. Israeli law authorizes people in those territories to carry a gun for protection. Within Israel proper, the laws are more stringent. Gun carriers must be licensed, and must convince authorities they have a valid reason for going armed. Also, guns must be registered.

Until the 1990s, laws were looser. Virtually any army veteran could get a gun license with no hassle. But in 1992, a security guard went on a rampage and killed four women at a mental-health clinic in Jerusalem. That led to increased sharing of information among government agencies, in an attempt to block people with mental-health problems from getting gun licenses. It also led to new restrictions, such as a law requiring the confiscation of guns from abusive spouses and a law requiring gun owners to demonstrate proficiency with their weapons. The latter law made it harder for Israeli Arabs to qualify for gun licenses, since courses in shooting added to the cost of getting a gun and instructors sometimes refused to admit Arabs to the courses.

The assassination of Prime Minister Yitzhak Rabin in 1995 by a gunman using a handgun led to a further tightening of laws. The gunman had acquired the handgun legally while living in the occupied territories, but had neglected the requirement that he give it up when he moved back to Israel. That led to stiffer licensing restrictions, including a requirement that applicants in Israel proper convince authorities of a need to carry a gun. Applicants must also present an identity card, proof of residence, and proof of military service.

Roughly 300,000 Israeli civilians (in a population of 5.6 million) are licensed to have guns. Most of the weapons are handguns. Israel has a relatively low rate of crimes involving firearms—for example, only one murder in ten involves a gun.

Canada

During 2000, Canadian gun owners went one by one to local police stations to fill out an official form. Some gun owners signed the forms at shopping malls or shooting clubs. What were those forms? They were applications for a gun license. After December 31, 2000, it became illegal to have a gun in Canada without a license. The new national law was highly unpopular in western provinces like Alberta and Saskatchewan, and several provincial governments went to court in an attempt to block it. But the attempt failed. In June 2000 the Canadian Supreme Court declared the law constitutional, stating: "The regulation of guns as dangerous products is a valid purpose within the criminal law power."[2] By the New Year's Day deadline, 1.8 million Canadian gun owners had been licensed. Authorities estimated another 400,000 were in technical violation of the law. (Around 22 percent of Canadian households have guns, compared with about 40 percent in the United States.)

Licensing of gun owners was but one step in a tightening of Canadian gun controls that were already far stricter than those in the United States. A second step was set for December 31, 2002, by which date all guns were required to be registered. The new gun laws can be traced back to national revulsion against a 1989 mass murder in which a man with a semiautomatic rifle killed fourteen women at a Montreal college.

Canada has a long history of gun controls, reflected in the following timeline. Polls show that about 70 percent of Canadians approve of gun control, while other Canadians adamantly oppose it.

1877 Anyone carrying a handgun without reasonable cause can be sent to jail for up to six months by a local justice of the peace.

1892 A nationwide permit system was established for people wanting to carry or sell small arms.

1932 A minimum sentence of two years was established for possessing or using a handgun in the commission of a crime.

1934 Handgun registration was required for the first time. Applicants had to state a reason for wanting a handgun.

1938 A person using *any* firearm in a crime became subject to a two-year minimum sentence.

1951 Registration of automatic firearms was begun, using a centralized registry.

1977 The purchaser of a firearm was required to get a Firearm Acquisition Certificate before taking possession of the gun.

1991 A 28-day waiting period was established for purchases of firearms. Buyers had to take safety training. Penalties for firearm crimes were increased. Controls on high-power and military-style firearms were toughened.

1996 Ten specific firearms crimes were made subject to yet tougher mandatory penalties.

2001 All gun owners were required to get licenses.

2003 All firearms to be registered.

Source: "Focus on Firearms," Canadian Firearms Centre, www.cfc-ccaf. gc.ca/research/pamplets/pdfs/focus-en.pdf.

U.S. gun-rights activists found it hard to understand Canadians' acquiescence to such far-reaching gun controls. But Canada has a history and a culture that differ in many ways from those of the United States. To start with, eighteenth-century Canadians did not rebel against far-away British rulers as people in the thirteen colonies did. Many American colonists who opposed the U.S. War of Independence sought refuge from it in Canada. They were seeking not "life, liberty, and the pursuit of happiness" but peace, stability, and order. Canadians have developed a reputation (rightly or wrongly) for being more law-abiding and less ornery than people of the United States. However, as in the United States, there is a divide in Canada between urban and rural portions of society. Gun rights is a hot-button political issue on the prairies and in the mountain provinces of the west, while gun control is far more popular in the urban eastern provinces.

Canada's gun controls had previously been tightened in 1976, when handguns were restricted. Under the 1976 law, anyone wanting to buy a handgun had to get a police permit that would be granted only for specific purposes. Permits were granted to law-enforcement officers, security guards, members of gun clubs, and authentic gun collectors. People who wanted to own a gun for reasons of personal security were almost always turned down.

To many Canadians, the nation's strict gun controls are a prime reason why gun murders are rare in Canada. In 1998, for example, only 151 people were murdered with guns in Canada, compared to 9,300 in the United States. Toronto, a city of 4.7 million people, had just 17 firearms murders that year. Canada's overall murder rate (including methods other than guns) is about one third that of the United States.

In a nation where the police are viewed as ineffective at best and a public menace at worst, gun control has not prospered. Although sweeping gun-control proposals have received widespread attention in Brazil, critics of gun control have so far managed to prevent their adoption. One of the critics' most effective arguments is that without guns citizens cannot defend themselves against either criminals or the police. (In one notorious incident in 1993, hooded military police fired a hail of bullets at seventy-two impoverished street children sleeping on the steps of a church in Rio de Janeiro. Eight children died. The apparent reason for the attack: One of the boys had thrown a stone and hit a police officer.)

Certainly Brazil is a violent society. In one recent year the homicide rate was more than six times as high in Rio de Janeiro as in New York City. São Paulo is another violent city. One June, gunmen shot up a bar on São Paulo's outskirts and killed four women and three men. It was the city's twenty-eighth multiple shooting of the year—and the year was less than half over. Shootouts between police and drug gangs are common.

One key reason for Brazil's violence is the immense gap between rich and poor. Brazil itself is not a poor country—it has a relatively high per capita income and is the most industrialized nation in South America. But it has an immense reservoir of poor people who can contrast their desperate lives with the relative comfort of the middle class and the ostentatious wealth of the upper class. Other rapidly industrializing countries, such as Mexico and South Africa, also have extremely high levels of murder and other crimes.

In theory Brazilians must register their guns, but rela- tively few people do. By one recent estimate, only 1.5 million of the 20 million guns in the country are registered. In recent years Brazil has attempted to seriously tighten its regulations on firearms. In 1999, for example, the state of Rio de Janeiro attempted to ban all sales of guns and ammunition except to police departments and security companies. Brazil's Supreme Court overturned that state law as unconstitutional, saying only the national government had the power to regulate firearms. At the time, the national legislature was considering a bill that would not only ban all firearms sales but would also require gun owners to turn in their guns. Even antique firearms would have to be turned in. Brazil has a strong gun-manufacturing industry (one of the largest in the world), and lobbyists for the industry strongly opposed the bill. Year after year, the lobby and other gun-rights advocates have managed to keep the bill bogged down in Brazil's Congress.

South Africa

"South Africa's love affair with firearms makes America's seem tepid," a British newspaper wrote in 1999. Guns are widely available in South Africa and often used for killing people, among other things. Indeed, South Africa has a gun death rate (including homicides, suicides, and accidents) almost twice that of the United States. Many AK-47s and other military rifles have made their way into South Africa from war-torn African countries like Angola and Congo. They often turn up in the hands of street gangs and drug dealers.

During the 1990s, South Africa had a loose system of gun licensing that allowed almost anyone to get a gun for any reason. However, after extensive and bitter debate, the legislature passed a tough gun-control law in November 2000. Among other things, the Firearms Control Act (phased in over a five-year period) requires gun owners to show why they need a gun. They must also take a test demonstrating that they know how to use firearms. Furthermore, the law limits to one the number of guns a person can have for self-defense. (Guns for hunting and sport shooting are not limited to one.) And the law sets the minimum age for gun ownership at twenty-one, up from sixteen. Gun licenses must be renewed every five years. South Africa bans fully automatic assault rifles, armor-piercing bullets, and realistic toy guns. Violations of the gun-control law can bring stiff fines (as much as $13,500) and up to twenty-five years in prison.

An alliance of three South African opposition parties harshly criticized the 2000 law. The critics claimed that the law penalized law-abiding South Africans and took away their right to self-defense. Some South Africans worried that the law gave too much power to the dominant African National Congress party, which first came to power in 1994, after a prolonged struggle against the white-imposed, racist system of apartheid.

Australia

Australia, too, has tightened its gun laws in recent years, partly in response to a 1996 gun massacre in the island state of Tasmania. In that incident, a man opened fire with an AR-15 semiautomatic rifle at a seaside resort, killing thirty-five men, women, and children and wounding eighteen more. Not that the laws were particularly lax before that. Australia's states and territories had required that all handguns be registered and all firearms owners be licensed. Further restrictions provided that handgun owners had to belong to a recognized gun club and that they could carry their handguns only from their home to a gun range or a gun shop.

Under tighter restrictions introduced in 1996 and 1997, all firearms, including rifles and shotguns, must now be registered. Assault weapons are outlawed, as are repeating-style rifles and shotguns. Moreover, in applying for a gun license, people must demonstrate that they have a "genuine reason and need" for owning a firearm. They must also take safety training. Using the proceeds from a one-time surcharge on the Australian income tax, the central government bought some 600,000 firearms from Australian gun owners.

The effects of the latest restrictions were hotly disputed. Citing statistics for 1997 from the Australian government, the Sporting Shooters Association of Australia claimed that gun-related homicides and armed robberies rose sharply after the stricter gun controls went into effect. The director of the Australian Institute of Criminology disputed that interpretation. Later research for his organization showed a decline in firearms-related deaths in Australia for 1997 and 1998. The figures do fluctuate from year to year, but the trend has been downward since the late 1980s.

More than two thirds of Australian gun deaths are suicides and about one fifth are homicides. Compared with the United States, where almost two thirds of all murders involve guns, Australia has a relatively low incidence of gun murders, with only one homicide in four involving a gun. The rate of gun homicides per 100,000 people is about fourteen times higher in the United States than in Australia.

One study of firearms homicides in Australia found that the weapons used were mainly handguns, and that the proportion of murders involving handguns had increased after the 1996–1997 law changes. The researcher suggested that this was because it had become harder to acquire rifles and shotguns legally, and because handguns were easily traded on the black market and easy to conceal. Most of the guns used in homicides were unregistered or had been stolen from a legitimate owner or had been illegally modified.

Because of this, the researcher concluded, further restrictions on gun ownership might do little to lower Australia's homicide rates. A better approach, the researcher stated, would be to crack down on illegal arms dealers and enforce laws that require legal owners of firearms to store their guns securely.

International Arms Traffic

In countries that have experienced civil wars or rebellions, governments are often too weak to enforce simple traffic laws, let alone gun controls. Many military weapons and small arms have fallen into the hands of bandits and terrorists. Other weapons have been retained by former combatants or are for sale on city streets and in rural markets. In addition, shady international arms dealers and official government arms agencies alike find ready buyers for shipments of weapons such as assault rifles and grenade launchers. The abundance of small arms contributes to

further rebellions and lawlessness in many of the world's
countries.

In the summer of 2001, the United Nations sponsored a conference in New York to consider ways of restricting the spread of such weapons. Delegates attended from more than 170 nations, including the United States. They tried to agree on rules to control the international traffic in small arms, defined as arms that can be transported and used by a single individual—from handguns and rifles to grenades and shoulder-launched missiles.

The conference stirred strong opposition among gun-rights activists in the United States. They saw the conference as an attempt to impose gun control on a worldwide scale, or in the words of National Rifle Association leader Wayne LaPierre, "global disarmament—disarming citizens worldwide—including you and me."[3] Stressing that he was not defending "trafficking stolen military arms to rogue armies and terrorists," LaPierre argued that "the U.N. draws no distinction between a missile launcher and your shotgun. To them, a bazooka and your Browning [rifle, shotgun, or pistol] are both 'small arms.'"[4]

But gun-control supporters strongly favored the conference. They backed calls from most of the world's nations for binding commitments to stop the traffic in small arms, arguing that illicit arms sales nurture dozens of conflicts that kill more than 500,000 people each year, 80 percent of whom are women and children. California Senator Dianne Feinstein, a Democrat, was part of the U.S. delegation to the conference. She spoke in favor of a treaty that would make possible the international tracing of weapons and greater "transparency" or openness in records of gun sales.

The U.S. government refused to accept parts of a draft proposal that called for countries to "seriously consider the prohibition of unrestricted trade and private ownership of small arms and light weapons specifically designed for military purposes."[5] Undersecretary of State John Bolton declared: "The United States believes that the responsible use of firearms is a legitimate aspect of national life."[6] He told the conference: "The United States will not join consensus on a final document that contains measures contrary to our constitutional right to keep and bear arms."[7]

In the end, the United States had its way. The conference dropped the proposal to restrict civilian possession of small arms. It also abandoned a proposal to bar arms sales to rebel groups and other "non-state actors," after the United States argued that to do so would interfere with support for "freedom fighters" against repressive regimes. (Both those measures had strong support from most other nations.) But the conference did reach agreement on a nonbinding plan for cracking down on the illicit trade in small arms. It called on governments to require manufacturers to mark small arms with unique identifiers and to keep records allowing such weapons to be traced. It also called for effective government regulation of small-arms sales and of the brokers who arrange such sales. Finally, the delegates agreed to hold a follow-up conference by 2006.

In many ways, the United States is unique in its approach to gun ownership and gun control. That uniqueness results from historical and cultural factors that have been at work for centuries. Many other nations have gone much further than the United States in seeking to restrict people's access to firearms. Today, depending on one's perspective, the United States can be seen either as laggard and out of step in the world's efforts to control gun violence, or as a stalwart defender of individual rights (and especially gun rights) against the dangers of oppressive governmental controls.

CHAPTER 8

Seeking Common Ground

On a mild morning in Denver in March 2000, gun-control and gun-rights people met the press together in a rare moment of unity. At a news conference, James Brady, for whom the Brady Law is named, and Wayne LaPierre, of the National Rifle Association, joined in praising Colorado's adoption of a get-tough-on-gun-crime plan called Project Exile. Started in 1997 in Richmond, Virginia, Project Exile has federal attorneys take the lead over state officials in prosecuting gun crimes, taking advantage of stiff penalties provided in federal laws. A felon who is caught with a

A billboard warns would-be offenders of
Project Exile's get-tough-on-crime measures.

firearm faces five years in prison—or fifteen years for committing a crime while carrying a gun—without possibility
of pardon or parole. In Colorado, U.S. Attorney Tom
Strickland explained: "The basic premise . . . is to take every
gun crime and refer it to the jurisdiction [federal, state, or
local] that can hit the bad guy the hardest."[1]

NRA leaders support Project Exile because it gets
criminals off the streets; gun-control backers such as
James Brady like the program because it keeps guns out of
"the wrong hands." In Richmond, supporters gave Project
Exile a large share of the credit for a 65 percent drop in

gun crime over a three-year period (although others sug- gested the crime drop had broader causes, including the elimination of parole).

Project Exile has been adopted statewide in Virginia, Texas, Colorado, and a few other states. It has also been adopted locally in cities like Rochester and Philadelphia. In 2000 the U.S. House of Representatives voted to finance a nationwide version of Project Exile, but the bill died in the Senate. President George W. Bush later proposed a $50 million federal-state program along similar lines.

Support for Project Exile is not unanimous, though. Under President Bill Clinton, the Department of Justice showed little enthusiasm for the program, preferring to focus federal attention on larger crimes. Moreover, some people criticize Project Exile as a waste of money, since federal prosecutions tend to be more costly than state or local ones. Some see it also as racist, claiming that it is more often used in metropolitan areas with large minority populations than in rural areas with mainly white populations. And some gun-rights supporters see it as a two-edged sword that can be used to enforce what they call "onerous gun laws" such as bans on certain rifles and high-capacity ammunition magazines.

Still, the fact that at least some gun-rights and gun-control advocates were able to agree on anything evoked surprise and hope in many observers. It was a sign that the two sides shared at least a few underlying concerns and values. Was it also, perhaps, a portent of future compromise, of some larger shared purpose that might replace the harsh rhetoric and bad feelings that have so often driven the two sides into warring camps? If nothing else, it offered a glimpse of an alternative reality.

In their day-to-day sparring, the gun-rights and gun-control sides seem to have nothing in common. They paint the world in blacks and whites, proclaiming their rival absolutes: that guns are a God-given (or at least constitutionally blessed) right, and that the road to national salvation lies through the elimination of gun violence.

Each camp seems to think it has truth—and the public—on its side. Opinion polls reveal some interesting nuances about public feelings. For example, large majorities consistently support stricter gun controls and believe that the easy availability of handguns is a major contributor to violence in the United States. Yet an even larger majority blames violence on a lack of adult supervision of children.

While poll results have varied somewhat over the years, the support for stricter gun controls has been high. Harris and Gallup polls report majorities of 54 percent to 70 percent in support of gun controls. But those bare figures mask the fact that men are far less likely than women to support stricter controls. In a recent Harris Poll, 51 percent of men and 72 percent of women favored stricter gun controls, while 31 percent of men and 14 percent of women wanted to make gun controls less strict. The same question revealed variations among other demographic groups. For example, the higher a person's level of education, the more that person tended to want stricter gun control. You might think that people with higher incomes would fall into the same category, but the highest income groups were somewhat less likely than the lowest income groups to favor stricter controls (59 percent vs. 69 percent).

When the Pew Research Center for the People and the Press (an independent opinion-research group) asked whether it was more important to protect the right to own guns or to control gun ownership, 46 percent of the men questioned and 67 percent of the women questioned favored gun controls, while 49 percent of the men and 28 percent of the women supported gun rights. Respondents in the East were the least likely to favor gun rights and the most likely to favor gun controls. Republicans favored gun rights over gun controls by 50 percent to 46 percent, while Democrats supported gun controls over gun rights by 67 percent to 28 percent.

Pollsters have also asked people for opinions about specific gun-control laws. Here are the percentages from selected polls in 1999 or later for people who support a proposed law:

To require mandatory sentences for felons who commit crimes with guns	89%
To require background checks for firearms sales at gun shows	87%
To require safety locks or trigger guards on new handguns	85%
To require a police permit prior to gun purchase	80%
To require registration of all firearms	79%
To ban importation of high-capacity ammunition clips	68%
To ban the manufacture, sale, or possession of semiautomatic assault rifles	59%

| To hold parents legally responsible if their children commit gun crimes | 57% |
| To ban the possession of handguns | 36% |

Polls also are useful in determining how many households own guns. Around 40 percent of those questioned say they keep a gun at home, and most of those people have more than one gun. About one fifth of gun owners have at least five guns. Why do people choose to own guns? Armed Americans say they want guns for three main purposes: target shooting (67 percent), protection against crime (65 percent), and hunting (59 percent).

The Role of the Media

With polls generally favorable to the gun-control advocates, why haven't they had more success in legislating their goals? That's a sore point with many gun-control supporters. They note, of course, the great energy of the gun-rights movement, especially the NRA with its lobbying arm, the Institute for Legislative Action (ILA). "The extremist gun lobby will continue to hold our nation hostage unless we mobilize and build an army of supporters to counter them," the Brady Campaign to Prevent Gun Violence has said. Gun-control supporters also perceive the gun manufacturing industry as an influential and antagonistic force. The political power of the gun-rights movement is spread over many states, especially rural states in the South, Midwest, and West and industrial states like Connecticut where gun manufacturing is concentrated. Gun-control advocates tend to lament the fact that the people most affected by gun violence—the urban poor—have relatively little political power and thus have traditionally had only a limited voice in the debate over gun control. If only such people could develop a stronger voice, the feeling goes, they could add to the political pressure for gun control.

The gun-rights side, too, sees the urban poor as a natural constituency. Who needs a gun for self-defense more than the resident of a crime-ridden urban neighborhood? But gun-rights supporters often express exasperation at the attractiveness of gun control to a significant part of the public. Is the nation losing its moral backbone? Have Americans abandoned the independent spirit and, yes, the orneriness of their ancestors? Have they been bought off by the lure of the welfare state? Lulled by the belief that the threat of tyranny went out with George III and the British redcoats?

Those who answer "yes" to questions like these often assign the blame to "the lying media," the newspapers and newsmagazines and television networks perceived as mouthpieces for liberal (read: anti–gun-rights) propaganda. The media come under regular and frequent attack in gun-rights publications, on gun-rights Web sites, and in speeches by gun-rights leaders. In an address at Yale University in 1999, NRA president Charlton Heston accused the mass media of collaborating with then-President Clinton to help pass unnecessary gun laws and then covering up the government's failure to use those laws. As an example, Heston cited the 1994 ban on certain semiautomatic firearms. He stated that "nobody is reporting that, out of thousands of certain offenders," the Clinton administration prosecuted just eight people under the act over a two-year period. Heston went on: "Nobody's getting arrested, nobody's going to jail, it's all a giant scam. It's not real life. It's a big lie, packaged by an alliance between this Administration and a media that systematically propagates its doctrine."[2] Gun-control supporters have their own bones to pick with the media. They accuse the entertainment industry, in particular, of glamorizing guns and violence. Reacting to one of the school shootings of the 1990s, Sarah Brady declared: "A nation that glorifies guns should not be shocked when children act out their darkest fantasies with those very same weapons."[3] A gun-control spokesman from Scotland carried the thought further: "It certainly seems to be the case that our entertainment and news media make guns desirable," he said. "But it's only our gun laws which make them available."[4]

The strong distrust of the news media shown by gun-rights supporters complicates the search for compromise over gun issues. While some criticisms of news coverage certainly have merit, others reveal a misunderstanding of the role of the media in modern society. News stories, after all, are descriptions of actual events taking place in the world around us. We expect the news media to take a fair-minded approach to events and issues, presenting a range of facts and interpretations that give all sides their due. But each story touches on only a small part of much bigger issues. Any one story or program may appear to lean to one side or another—raising points that seem inconvenient or dubious to partisans with strongly held views but that deserve an airing nonetheless. On the one side, gun-rights supporters often feel that the media pay too much attention to eruptions of gun mayhem like the Columbine High School shootings. On the other side, gun-control advocates might prefer not to hear about research findings that suggest a new gun-control law has had little effect on holding down gun accidents or gun crimes. It is all too easy to let one's ideology blind one to the many facets of a complex issue like gun control—to see bias just because one's own point of view is not used as the basis for an assessment.

In the Internet age, an added danger lurks in the shadows. It is so easy now to gorge oneself on like-minded opinions and purported facts from Web sites or discussion forums that focus so completely on one point of view that they demonize rival readings of public issues. The slogan "All who are not with us are against us" quickly morphs into "If you disagree with us, you are our enemy" and perhaps ". . . you are a traitor to our way of life." Even partisans need to hear rival viewpoints now and then in order to be able to construct persuasive arguments—arguments that might win others to their cause. "Many people are now using the Internet so as to strengthen what they already believe—and to fence out different or opposing positions," observes Cass Sunstein, a University of Chicago professor. ". . . When people hear and read views with which they already agree, they tend to go to extremes, and often to demonize, or misunderstand, their fellow citizens."[5] Sunstein has written a book, *Republic.com,* about this phenomenon, which he and other social scientists call "group polarization."

Costs and Benefits

Some sort of dialogue across ideological boundaries will be needed if the gap between rival sides on gun-related issues is to be bridged. One fruitful approach might be for the two sides to cooperate in assessing the impact of existing gun-control laws and pro–gun-rights legislation. Has the 1994 Brady Law paid off on its promise to reduce gun crimes and keep guns out of the hands of criminals? Have "concealed carry" laws that expand gun owners' rights to go armed been effective at deterring criminals and saving lives? Social scientists have been churning out studies for years about gun ownership, guns and crime, gun laws and crime, gun accidents, and so on—but each side has tended to interpret the studies in ways that support its own position. By now there are plenty of statistics. Perhaps it is time for a good-faith effort by the rival sides to explore the findings together and look for areas of potential agreement. Who knows? It just might be possible to nudge the rivals toward some sort of compromise on future legislative goals.

A common approach to weighing the advantages and disadvantages of a proposed policy is to draw up two lists. One list shows the expected benefits of the policy. The other shows the problems it might cause—its disadvantages, or costs. Applied to a hypothetical gun-control law, for example, such a *cost/benefit analysis* might show that gun owners would have to pay, say, $600 million a year to equip their guns with new safety devices such as locks. That amount goes on the *cost* side of the balance. A predicted number of injuries or deaths that might come about if gun locks prevented defensive gun use in an emergency could also go on the cost side. On the *benefit* side might be an expected saving of, say, fifty lives (people who would otherwise die of gun injuries) plus an anticipated saving on medical care for gun injuries. A value would be assigned to each life lost or saved and those amounts would be added to the other costs and benefits. In the end, if the total benefits outweigh the total costs, the proposal makes economic sense. But if the costs exceed the benefits, the proposal fails this economic test.

Of course, money issues are only part of the big picture, and some proposals succeed or fail on other
grounds. The idea that the right to own guns is constitutionally protected is not easily reduced to a dollars-and-
cents analysis. Neither is the belief that it is more
important to save innocent lives than to cater to those
with a passion for guns.

Indeed, some observers believe that unstated assumptions on both the gun-control and gun-rights sides make
their differences almost impossible to bridge. Their view
goes something like this:

- On the one hand, many gun-control advocates operate
  from the assumption that armed self-defense has no
  place in a settled and civilized twenty-first-century society. For this reason, some gun-control advocates want
  to ban guns altogether—at the very least, handguns.

- On the other hand, gun-rights supporters tend to
  assume that *all* gun-control advocates ultimately favor
  an outright ban on guns. Therefore, they ask: Why compromise? Each step toward gun control is a step closer
  to the prohibition of all guns. Besides, many gun-rights
  supporters believe that the principle of armed self-
  defense can *never* be a subject for compromise.

The debate over assault weapons provides one
example. Gun-control supporters say (1) assault guns
are a weapon of choice for mass killings; (2) assault
guns are not useful for sports; (3) thus, there is no legitimate purpose for assault guns; (4) therefore, assault
guns must be banned. Gun-rights supporters say (1)
any gun can be misused; (2) both sports and self-
defense are legitimate uses of guns; (3) assault guns are

A robber grabs your handgun away from you and aims it at your chest. Do you panic? No way! Your gun is a "smart gun" that won't shoot for anyone but you. As you race merrily away, you shout back, "So long, sucker." The unlucky robber is gazing down the barrel, still trying to get the gun to shoot.

That is the scenario painted by supporters of a variety of gizmos designed to require guns to "identify" their owner before loosening up for a shot. Besides protecting gun owners whose guns have been grabbed away, such devices would keep children from accidentally firing their daddy's (or mommy's) gun. Very few of these devices seem to be ready for prime time. But given the amount of money and energy going into their development, it may be only a matter of time.

The gun industry has been trying a number of different approaches. One of the most exotic devices would prevent a gun from operating until it heard and identified the voice of its owner. (What would the owner say? Perhaps: "You may fire when you are ready, Gridley"—famously spoken by U.S. Commodore George Dewey to a subordinate at the start of the Spanish-American War.) Another device would read the fingerprint of the digit touching the trigger. If it matched the owner's fingerprint, the gun would fire. No match—no boom. Still another device would keep a gun locked until it was activated by a magnetic ring on the gun owner's trigger finger. (A clever child armed with a refrigerator magnet might foil this one, critics say.) And another device would require a small, handheld radio transmitter to activate a gun.

"Smart guns" are a high-tech version of more traditional trigger locks that have been available for years. Some gun makers, like Smith & Wesson, offer guns with built-in trigger locks that open with a small key. Mechanical devices of this sort are popular among gun users with small children in the home, and some states now require them. But they are decidedly low-tech, and they require time to unlock. The appeal of "smart guns" is that they seem to offer an almost instant response when used by the authorized person.

But critics see many flaws in the "smart gun" idea. Devices that depend on voice or fingerprint recognition or radio signals require batteries, and batteries run down. If you leave a gun in a drawer for years without checking its batteries, you may grab it one night to defend yourself and find that it no longer works. Magnetic devices don't use batteries, but refrigerator magnets can be found in almost every house and carried by bad guys as well as gun owners. And besides, if you're wearing a magnetic ring, you can accidentally erase the data on a credit card or a cassette tape.

Other problems abound. Your gun can't recognize your fingerprint if you're wearing a glove—or if your finger is smudged or you grab the trigger at the wrong angle. As for voice recognition, would your frightened squawk in an emergency sound anything like the normal voice you have trained your gun to recognize? Some people think not.

The original impetus behind "smart guns" was a desire to protect the lives of police officers. Half a dozen or more officers are killed each year when someone grabs their gun and fires. The National Institute of Justice began financing research on "smart guns" in 1994. Many designs have been too bulky or too complex, so research continues.

Gun-control advocates have been enthusiastic supporters of "smart gun" research, and in some states they have pushed for legislation to require "smart" safety devices on guns for sale. So far, the technology is just not ready. Gun-rights organizations claim that requiring high-tech safety devices would cost from $300 to $900 per gun, and accuse gun-control groups of seeking to make guns too costly for the average user. As the gun-rights people see it, government "should not require consumers to purchase products that they do not want or feel they do not need."

appropriate for self-defense; (4) therefore, assault guns must be permitted.

Even if cost/benefit analysis could be expanded to take such noneconomic issues into account, there still would be the problem of unexpected consequences. Even the most detailed analysis is not a crystal ball. Almost always a change in the law brings some surprising outcomes. For example, during the 1980s and 1990s, criminal laws were toughened with features such as mandatory minimum sentences and "three strikes and out" laws that set extremely long sentences (even life imprisonment) for third convictions. A case can be made that such tougher laws helped to reduce crime by putting career criminals behind bars. But there were other consequences as well. Law-enforcement officers discovered that the laws increased their risk of getting shot, as cornered suspects facing long prison terms became less likely to give themselves up and more likely to shoot to kill. Some critics of gun control worry that stricter gun laws might also have unintended consequences. Would such laws be widely ignored, as happened during the era of Prohibition, when a ban on alcohol sales opened the way for bootlegging and a vast expansion of criminal enterprises?

Costs and benefits also enter into discussions about the Second Amendment and other parts of the Bill of Rights. Oddly, though, liberals and conservatives tend to switch sides when they move from rights such as freedom of speech and the right to due process, to the right to keep and bear arms. On most parts of the Bill of Rights, liberals stress a respect for individual rights even when the potential cost to society is high. For example, when it comes to the Fifth Amendment right to keep silent and not testify against oneself in a criminal case, liberals tend

to argue that it is better for a criminal to escape punish-
ment than for an innocent person to be convicted. In other words, they would err on the side of rights. Conservatives, in contrast, tend to want to minimize the costs to society and thus are more likely to accept restraints on the Fifth Amendment right to avoid self-incrimination or, say, the First Amendment right to freedom of speech. But when it comes to the Second Amendment, it is conservatives who seek an expansive interpretation of an individual's right to keep and bear arms. Liberals, on this issue, are the ones who stress the costs to society of easy access to firearms and who would prefer to place restrictions on individual rights.

There are, in fact, people on both sides who can see some justice in what the other side is saying. Warren Burger was a conservative stalwart who served as Chief Justice of the United States from 1969 to 1986. Yet he supported some forms of gun control and went so far as to accuse the gun lobby of perpetrating fraud on the American people by claiming that the Second Amendment guarantees an unconditional right to bear arms. On the other side, liberal University of Texas professor Sanford Levinson calls himself "a card-carrying ACLU member who doesn't own a gun." Yet he wrote an article (widely circulated by NRA members) affirming that the Second Amendment limits the government's power to regulate gun ownership.

If we look closely, we can see possible areas of agreement between these two—the conservative who sees a place for gun control and the liberal who sees limits on the power to regulate guns. The devil is in the details, though. How many controls on guns? How much regulation? Where to draw the line between individual rights and public safety?

In the end, perhaps the focus needs to be on the problems and concerns of individuals whose lives have been touched by guns. People like Edward Prince, whose nineteen-year-old son, a college student, was shot during a robbery. In testimony before Congress during consideration of the Brady Bill, Prince asked rhetorically: "Was that a well-trained militia that killed my son?"[6]

And we might also remember the power of an armed and angry citizenry. In colonial Virginia, Governor Sir William Berkeley was well aware of that power. On the eve of the 1676 colonists' uprising we know as Bacon's Rebellion, Berkeley wrote: "How miserable that man is . . . that Governes a People wher six parts of seaven at least are Poore Endebted Discontented and Armed."[7] The rebellion was a failure, but it certainly caught the governor's attention.

SOURCE NOTES

TO OUR READERS: All the Internet addresses in this book were active and correct when the book went to press.

Chapter 2

1. John M. Broder, "Clinton Orders Study on Selling of Violence," *The New York Times*, June 2, 1999.

2. Kevin Flynn, "Heston Indignant, Defiant," *Rocky Mountain News*, May 2, 1999, p. A20.

3. Fox Butterfield, "Are Gun Laws, and Agency That Enforces Them, Equal to the Task?" *The New York Times*, July 22, 1999, p. A1.

4. Wayne R. LaPierre, *Guns, Crime, and Freedom* (Washington, DC: Regnery Publishing, 1994), p. 177. When the NRA used the term "jack-booted thugs" in a fund-raising letter in 1995, it stirred up such a storm of criticism that former President George H. W. Bush resigned from the NRA in protest.

5. LaPierre, p. 197.

6. See U.S. Senate, Report of the Senate Judiciary Committee Subcommittee on the Constitution, 97th Cong., 2d Sess., "The Right to Keep and Bear Arms," Committee Print I–IX, 1–23 (1982), available online at www.2ndlawlib.org/other/other/senrpt/.

7. Fox Butterfield, "Guns: The Law As Selling Tool," *The New York Times*, August 13, 2000, section 4, p. 4.

8. Butterfield, "Are Gun Laws, and Agency That Enforces Them, Equal to the Task?"

Chapter 3

1. Russ Chastain, "What Makes a Gun Lover?" January 4, 2001, http://hunting.about.com/recreation/hunting/library/weekly/aa010104.htm.

2. U.S. Department of the Interior, Fish and Wildlife Service and U.S. Department of Commerce, Bureau of the Census, *1996 National Survey of Fishing, Hunting, and Wildlife—Assoicated Recreation,* pp. 103–104

3. Quoted on www.abcnews.go.com/sections/us/guns/guns_romance.html.

4. *Philadelphia Daily News,* June 4, 1998, story by Mark Angeles, accessed online at http://interactive.philly.com/content/dailynews.backup/98/Jun/04/local?NRAA04.htm, but no longer available there.

Chapter 4

1. Sarah Brady, ". . . And the Case Against Them . . . The Head of Handgun Control Says Weapons Are Killing the Future," *Time*, January 29, 1990, p. 23, excerpted in Marjolijn Bijlefeld, ed., *The Gun Control Debate: A Documentary History* (Westport, CT: Greenwood Press, 1997), p. 109.

1. Quoted in Charles P. Cozic, ed., *Gun Control*. Current Controversies series (Westport, CT: Greenwood Press, 1992), p. 59.
2. Robert Sherrill, *The Saturday Night Special: and Other Guns with Which Americans Won the West, Protected Bootleg Franchises, Slew Wildlife, Robbed Countless Banks, Shot Husbands Purposely and by Mistake and Killed Presidents—Together with the Debate Over Continuing Same* (New York: Charterhouse, 1973), p. 280.
3. Wayne LaPierre, *Guns, Crime, and Freedom* (Washington, DC: Regnery Publishing, 1994), p. 167.
4. Quoted in Jorgen Wouters, "The Land of Guns and Death" at www.abcnews.go.com/sections/us/guns/guns_romance.html.
5. Gary Kleck, Summary of *Point Blank: Guns and Violence in America* (1991), excerpted as Document 150 in Marjolijn Bijlefeld, ed., *The Gun Control Debate: A Documentary History* (Westport, CT: Greenwood Press, 1997), p. 174. Full summary is available online at www.tuxedo.org/~esr/guns/point-blank-summary.html.
6. J. Neil Schulman, "Talk at Temple Beth Shir Shalom," in Jan E. Dizard, Robert Merrill Muth, and Stephen P. Andrews Jr., eds., *Guns in America: A Reader* (New York: New York University Press, 1999), p. 405.
7. Billboard created by California Rifle and Pistol Association. An image of the billboard is available online at www.crpa.org/pressrls100101.html.
8. Brady Campaign press release, October 12, 2001, accessed online at www.bradycampaign.org/press/release.
9. Statement by NRA, September 27, 2001, available online at www.nraila.org/NewsCenter.

1. Quoted in Harry Henderson, *Gun Control.* Library in a Book series (New York: Facts On File, Inc., 2000), p. 11.
2. Paragraph 7 in second part of Bill of Rights, quoted in Henderson, p. 11.
3. *United States* v. *Miller,* 307 U.S. 174 (1939) (USSC+), Opinions, MCREYNOLDS, J., Opinion of the Court, available online at www2.law.cornell.edu/cgi-bin/foliocgi.exe/historic/query=miller+layton/doc/
4. *United States* v. *Miller.*
5. Quoted by NRA in "Word for Word: The Second Amendment Debate," *The New York Times,* September 24, 2000, section 4, p. 7. Source: *Debates and Other Proceedings of the Convention of Virginia,* convened at Richmond, on Monday the 2d day of June 1788 (Petersburg, VA: Printed by Hunter and Prentis, 1788), quoted in Wayne R. LaPierre, *Guns, Crime, and Freedom* (Washington, DC: Regnery Publishing, Inc., 1994), pp. 16–17 (footnote p. 243).
6. "The Right to Keep and Bear Arms," Report of the Subcommittee on the Constitution of the United States Senate, 97th Congress, Second Session, February 1982, available online at www.constitution.org/mil/rkba1 982.htm.
7. *Annals of Congress,* Vol. 1, p. 451, June 8, 1789, quoted in Carl Bakal, *The Right to Bear Arms* (McGraw-Hill Book Company, 1966), p. 303.
8. The Wisconsin constitution is available online at www.legis.state.wi.us/rsb/2wiscon.html.
9. The Alaska constitution is available online at www.gov. state.ak.us/ltgov/akcon/table.html.
10. *United States* v. *Emerson,* Criminal Action No. 6:98-CR-103-C (U.S. District Court for the Northern District of Texas, San Angelo Division, 1999), available online at news.find law.com/cnn/docs/gunlawsuits/emerson/emerson.pdf, pp. 5 and 27.

11. *United States* v. *Emerson* (99-10331), 5th Cir. 2001 (rendered
    October 16, 2001), accessed online at www.ca5.uscourts.
    gov/opinions/getopin.cfm?loc=99/99-10331-cr0.htm.
12. Quoted in Charles Lane, "U.S. Court Upholds Ownership
    of a Gun as Constitutional Right," *Washington Post,* Octo-
    ber 17, 2001, p. A17.
13. *Dred Scott* v. *Sandford,* 60 U.S. (19 How.), 417, 1857,
    excerpted in Marjolijn Bijlefeld, ed., *The Gun Control
    Debate: A Documentary History* (Westport, CT: Greenwood
    Press, 1997), pp. 44–45.

Chapter 7

1. Brady Campaign, "Firearm Facts," available online at
   www.bradycampaign.org/facts/research/firefacts.asp.
   Footnote says "Foreign data provided by each country's
   embassy. Data for the United States from: Crime in the
   United States, 1996. Washington DC. Federal Bureau of
   Investigation. 1997. The number for Germany represents
   total murders by firearms."
2. Ruth Walker, "Canadian Provinces Threaten to Resist New
   Gun Law," *Christian Science Monitor,* June 30, 2000.
3. Wayne R. LaPierre, speech in St. Louis, quoted in "Odd
   Couples: Unusual Alliances Expected at Small Arms Conference," *Arms Trade News,* distributed by Middle East
   News Online, June 27, 2001, available online at www.mid-
   dleeastwire.com/world/stories/20010627_18_meno.shtml.
4. Quoted in Jim Burns, "LaPierre Reflects on Decade at
   NRA Helm," CNSNews.com (Cybercast News Service),
   May 21, 2001, available online at www.armed-citizens.
   com/news/armdcitz_news.php?doit=yes&newsid=520.
5. Quoted in Joshuah Bearman and Nick Rosen, "The gun
   lobby goes to war with the U.N., *L.A. Weekly,* July 13, 2001,
   online at dailynews.yahoo.com/h/laweekly/20010713/lo/
   26396_1.html.

6. Quoted in Barbara Crossette, "U.N. Effort to Cut Arms Traffic Meets a U.S. Rebuff," *The New York Times,* July 10, 2001, p. A8.

7. Quoted in Colum Lynch, "U.S. Fights U.N. Accord To Control Small Arms; Stance on Draft Pact Not Shared by Allies," *Washington Post*, July 10, 2001, p. A1.

Chapter 8

1. Quoted on Colorado Project Exile Web site at www.coloradoprojectexile.com/.

2. Charlton Heston, speech to Yale University Political Union, April 16, 1999, available online at www.nrahq. org/transcripts/yale.asp.

3. Sarah Brady, "Statement of Sarah Brady Re: Arkansas Schoolyard Killings," Handgun Control press release, March 25, 1998, available online at www.bradycampaign. org/press/ release.asp?Record=110, after Jonesboro school shootings.

4. Dr. Mick North (from Gun Control Network, Scotland), speaking at Hague Appeal for Peace seminar, The Hague, Netherlands, May 14, 1999, available online at www.pcvp. org/pcvp/ firearms/Intl/haguep.shtml.

5. Q & A on Princeton University Press Web site at http:// pup.princeton.edu/releases/m7014.html.

6. Quoted in Charles P. Cozic, ed., *Gun Control.* Current Controversies series (Westport, CT: Greenwood Press, 1992), p. 247.

7. Wilcomb E. Washburn, *The Goveror and the Rebel: a History of Bacon's Rebellion in Virginia* (Chapel Hill, NC: University of North Carolina Press [for The Institute of Early American History and Culture at Williamsburg], 1957), p. 31.

FURTHER READING

ABC News. *America's Dangerous Liaison with Firearms: The Land of Guns and Death.* Part one of three-part series, broadcast June 19, 1998. www.abcnews.go.com/sections/us/guns/guns_romance.html (with links to rest of series).

Bakal, Carl. *The Right to Bear Arms.* New York: McGraw-Hill Book Company, 1966.

Barnett, Randy E., and Don B. Kates. "Under Fire: The New Consensus on the Second Amendment." *Emory Law Journal,* volume 45 (1996), pp. 1139–1259. Available: www.2ndlawlib. org/journals/bk-ufire.html.

Bijlefeld, Marjolijn, ed. *The Gun Control Debate: A Documentary History.* Westport, CT: Greenwood Press, 1997.

Bureau of Alcohol, Tobacco and Firearms. "Firearms: Overview: Legal." [Links to extensive information about U.S. firearms law.] www.atf.treas.gov/firearms/legal/index.htm.

CBS News. *Armed America: Innocence Lost.* Part one of five-part series, broadcast July 13, 1999. Available: http://wfor.cbsnow.

com/now/story/0,1597,53725-412,00.shtml (with links to rest of series).

Cottrol, Robert J., ed. *Gun Control and the Constitution: Sources and Explorations on the Second Amendment.* Florence, KY: Garland Publishing, Inc., 1993.

Cramer, Clayton E. "The Racist Roots of Gun Control." *Kansas Journal of Law and Public Policy*, Winter 1995. Available: www.wizard.net/~kc/roots.htm.

Davidson, Osha Gray. *Under Fire: The NRA and the Battle for Gun Control.* New York: Henry Holt and Company, 1993.

Dizard, Jan E., Robert Merrill Muth, and Stephen P. Andrews Jr., eds. *Guns in America: A Reader.* New York: New York University Press, 1999.

Federal Bureau of Investigation. *National Instant Criminal Background Check System Fact Sheet.* Available: www.fbi.gov/hq/cjisd/nics/nicsfact.htm#top.

Gun Owners of California. *State Laws and Reciprocity Guides: State Gun Laws.* Available: http://gunownersca.com/RecpIndx.htm.

Hardy, David T. "The Firearms Owners' Protection Act: A Historical and Legal Perspective." *Cumberland Law Review*, volume 17 (1986), pp. 585–682. Available: www.2ndlawlib.org/journals/hardfopa.html.

Independence Institute. *Criminal Justice and the Second Amendment.* Links to Web collections and articles. http://i2i.org/crimjust.htm.

Kennett, Lee, and James LaVerne Anderson. *The Gun in America: The Origins of a National Dilemma.* Westport, CT: Greenwood Press, 1975.

Kopel, David B. "It Isn't About Duck Hunting: The British Origins of the Right to Arms." *Michigan Law Review*, volume 93

(1995), pp. 1333–1362; available www.2ndlawlib.org/jour-nals/dk-dhunt.html.

Malcolm, Joyce Lee. "Concealed Weapons: The Controversial Book *Arming America* Has the Facts All Wrong." *Reason* maga-zine, January 2001; available http://reason.com/0101/cr.jm.concealed.html.

Michigan State University Libraries. *Criminal Justice Resources: Gun Control.* Links to Web sites, articles, etc. www.lib.msu.edu/harris23/crimjust/guncont.htm.

National Rifle Association *A Citizen's Guide to Federal Firearms Laws.* www.nraila.org/GunLaws.asp?FormMode=Detail&ID=60.

Noble, Ron, and Dave Kopel. *Gun Control and Gun Rights.* Web links and syllabus for 1998 college course at New York Univer-sity; links to many sources. www.law.nyu.edu/ nobler/guncon trol/.

Sherrill, Robert. *The Saturday Night Special: And Other Guns with Which Americans Won the West, Protected Bootleg Franchises, Slew Wildlife, Robbed Countless Banks, Shot Husbands Purposely and by Mistake and Killed Presidents—Together with the Debate Over Contin-uing Same.* New York: Charterhouse, 1973.

United Nations Crime and Justice Information Network. *United Nations International Study on Firearm Regulation.* www.uncjin. org/Statistics/firearms/index.htm.

Wright, James D., and Peter H. Rossi. *Armed and Considered Dangerous: A Survey of Felons and Their Firearms.* New York: Aldine de Gruyter, 1986.

Wright, James D., Peter H. Rossi, Kathleen Daly, et al. *Under the Gun: Weapons, Crime, and Violence in America.* New York: Aldine Publishing Company, 1983.

Page numbers in *italics* refer to illustrations.